Mom,

Merry Christmas! Thank you for all your love for me! Thank you for taking me to church so that I could know the true meaning of Christmas!

Brenda

The

AMISH
BOOK
of
PRAYERS
FOR
WOMEN

The
AMISH
BOOK
of
PRAYERS
FOR
WOMEN

ESTHER STOLL

HARVEST HOUSE PUBLISHERS
EUGENE, OREGON

Cover by Dugan Design Group, Bloomington, Minnesota

Cover illustration © tandaleah / Bigstock

THE AMISH BOOK OF PRAYERS FOR WOMEN
Copyright © 2015 by Esther Stoll
Published by Harvest House Publishers
Eugene, Oregon 97402
www.harvesthousepublishers.com

ISBN 978-0-7369-6375-6 (pbk.)
ISBN 978-0-7369-6376-3 (eBook)

Printed in China

14 15 16 17 18 19 20 21 / RDS-JH / 10 9 8 7 6 5 4 3 2 1

*To those who share the desire to
lean wholly on our Heavenly Father*

Acknowledgments

I am deeply indebted to…

My Heavenly Father, for the provision He has made in giving me the gift of living for His glory and His pleasure.

My faithful husband, Philip, who cherishes me deeply as his wife and lives with me daily as a God-ordained husband is called to; and for his continuing encouragement in putting my thoughts on paper.

My precious children, Keith and Gloria, who bless and enrich our lives and homes daily.

My parents, Dan and Mattie, who bear the sweetest name and who brought me up in a Christian setting and care deeply about what happens in my life.

My brothers, David, Harvey, Wyman, and Reuben, and in-laws, Laura, Grace Ann, and Naomi, who are a big part of my life and are a great blessing to me.

All my sisters in Christ, who touch my life in so many ways and help me be the woman I am today.

Contents

1. Hearth and Home 9

2. Love, Joy, and Gratitude. 25

3. Friendship and Fellowship 59

4. Training the Heart 77

5. The Hearts of the Children. 125

6. The Bond of Marriage 145

7. Drawing Closer to God 157

1
Hearth and Home

Dear Father of Love and Mercy,

You delight in pouring Your Spirit into our hearts and homes. I thank You for that gift. Your eyes also run to and fro looking for homes to show Yourself strong (2 Chronicles 16:9). Thank You, Father, for being *for* us. You are for strong homes and close family ties, and who shall be against us? May You, Father, be manifested in each of our hearts and in our home. The goal, the visions, the dream of what my husband and I long for our home move us to draw closer to You and, with a new zeal, we set out to face the challenges of each new day, knowing the choices we make today will affect the generations to come. *Amen.*

◇◇◇◇

Father of Love and Mercy: thank You for the many gifts You have bestowed on us—the shelter we call our home, the stores of food from our own garden and farm, the gift of two healthy children who are so eager to learn and help in making our home a pleasant one. I am so blessed in always having enough to share with family and friends and all who pass our way. My desire, Father, is to be given to hospitality as was the woman of Shunem. *Amen.*

◇◇◇◇

Thank You, God, for choosing my father and mother to bring me into this world. I know it's not by chance, but by Your choosing that I am here at this time in history. May I in no way hinder Your purpose for me. And may I find a joy in fulfilling Your calling as a mother and wife and a servant for You. *Amen.*

◇◇◇◇

Thank You, Father of Heaven and Earth, for giving me such weighty work. You committed two of Your precious souls to our care, to nurture and admonish and lead back to You. Daily, hourly, and momently You give me important work: cleaning, baking, laundering, and being a witness and inspiration to those around me. May they see You as they observe me being about my Father's business. And may it be a daily joy and inspiration to my own life. *Amen.*

◇◇◇◇

Thank You, Loving Father and Lord of All. I praise You for the provision You have made for me, that You have given Your life that I might live. And You have done it even before I could ask. At times I fail, stumble, and fall. Of myself, I am nothing. And yet pride and fear have been too much a part of my life. May You continue to daily cleanse me, mold me, shape me, and do with me what You see fit. I also pray for my husband as he puts in another day of winning bread. May he be a shining light to all he meets. May he be richly blessed for his faithfulness. And for each of our children, I pray that You would guide their purity, and if destruction should fall on them in any way, that You would reveal it to us. And may they grow to build up Your kingdom. I give this day in Your charge. I trust that You will fight as we work and pray. *Amen.*

◇◇◇◇

Dear Heavenly Father, thank You for the work of the cross, for shedding Your blood for my redemption, in which I can now live a victorious life. My desire is to have my heart continually turned to You, putting away all strange gods and having a heart prepared unto You, that our household—our home and children—may be sealed in You and be delivered daily from the invading enemy. *Amen.*

◇◇◇◇

Dear Father in Heaven, thank You for choosing me for royal priesthood, for the gift of being able to continually direct our little souls to You. Thank You for giving us a home that's special, where the latest styles and fashions are not found, but where Your Spirit reigns richly. Our house is no mansion, yet to us it's the most wonderful place on earth. May our home show forth the praises of You, the One who called us out of darkness into His marvelous light (1 Peter 2:9b). *Amen.*

◇◇◇◇

Dear Heavenly Master, thank You for the gift of physical life, and above all, thank You for the gift of spiritual life, for breathing Your Spirit on me. May my heart be so conditioned that, as easily as I inhale and exhale the breath of physical life, I'm subconsciously inhaling and exhaling Your Spirit. May my husband and children enjoy the gift of having a Spirit-filled wife and mother. *Amen.*

◇◇◇◇

Dear Father of Good Gifts, thank You for the gift of health, and for a warm, comfortable house that has given many happy hours of cleaning, scrubbing, sorting, and setting everything in order. Thank You also for the effort our children put in, in making sorting an extra joy. Father, I take this time to ask You to do housecleaning in my heart. I invite You to do every corner, shelf, and closet. Convict me as You find something that saddens You and that would be a hindrance in having full fellowship with You. May I be washed clean in Your blood. *Amen.*

◇◇◇◇

Dear Father of Good and Perfect Gifts: this morning, I give You an extra thank-you for the gift of eating breakfast with my family every morning. Thank You that we have food aplenty. There are so many things to choose from—oatmeal, rice porridge, pancakes, eggs, breakfast burritos; then there are all kinds of fruits: strawberries, pears, peaches, mulberries, and apples. Our food supply is endless. Thank You, Father, is all I can say. I'm sure there are many mothers who wonder what they will serve for the next meal. As we gather for breakfast this morning, may I remember with a grateful heart what a blessed opportunity it is. And as we eat, remind me to do my part to make mealtimes lasting memories for our dear little ones. *Amen.*

◇◇◇◇

Dear Father of Love and Mercy: if others who pass by can see that salvation has come to our house, then I'm a happy woman. The last weeks I've been battling with discontentment. At this time, our house is smaller than most of the houses around us. With our creative little ones, our house looks cluttered in no time. We clean up and soon we have to start all over again. Thank You, Lord, that happiness doesn't depend on circumstances. And truly, Lord, if our household is a house of peace, a haven of rest, if salvation has come to dwell here, then what else could I long for? Jesus, I'm sure You didn't first pause and survey Zacchaeus's house to see if it was spotless, had matching sheet sets, and matching bathroom sets. No, it was his heart that You were looking at. May our household be worthy of Your salvation. *Amen.*

◇◇◇◇

Dear Father of Love and Shepherding: You know my desire, Father, to be discreet, chaste, a keeper at home, good, and obedient to my husband. I realize what a high calling motherhood is. I am humbled that You have given me such a weighty work of service. And yet I am grateful to You for the experience of being a mother to two precious souls and a wife to my husband. I know I have failed often, and yet I thank You for giving me the opportunity to get up and try again. May I be true to my calling, looking daily to You for my all. *Amen.*

◇◇◇◇

Dear Father of Truth, thank You for being my Father and showing me the way. Without You, I stumble and fail. May I, with a clear conscience, tell the children to follow me as I follow You. And may I be faithful in keeping the promise that I made to You and my husband the day we married. Thank You also for a faithful husband who is kind, gentle, and true, and who I find easy to respect and love. Even if he were quite the opposite, I know that, with You, it would still be possible to respect and reverence him the same. It would not change the promise I made. *Amen.*

◇◇◇◇

Dear Father of Heaven and Earth: I'm sorry how often I've been careless and unheeding to Your call. Only yesterday, I opened the window and hurled words of frustration and anger at my little brood, who were playing in a water puddle. They were dressed in their Sunday best, which added to my frustration. But Lord, I know that is no excuse. My little ones were hurt, and never can I retract those words. Thank You for forgiving me and giving me the opportunity to exercise a deeper dependence on You. Father, may I be more diligent in heeding Your call and Your warning, and seeking shelter lest our house be left desolate. *Amen.*

◇◇◇◇

Dear Father, thank You for blessing our home with Your little angels, who brighten every corner. Thank You for giving them healthy bodies so that they can enjoy Your world, which You have created for our pleasure. Thank You also for the miracle of spring thaw, a sure sign that winter and its harsh cold are now behind us and we are soon to witness the earth burst forth into life. For doesn't the cold make the warmth so much richer? The storms make the rainbow so much more beautiful? And the mud make the grass so much greener? Thank You, Father. *Amen.*

◇◇◇◇

Dear Father, thank You for being a lighthouse for Your people. You are a light that has been shining through the ages. Your light is bright enough to shine to the uttermost parts of the earth. You are our guidance, direction, our warmth and protection. May our home reflect that light. My desire is that our children and others find our home a haven of rest from the toil of this world—a place of peace, a light for their feet, guidance for their young souls. May they see that You dwell here. *Amen.*

◇◇◇◇

Good morning, Father: first of all, I praise You for who You are and for the love and patience and blessings You have bestowed on our home and family. You know my heart's desire to be the mother You want me to be to our little ones. Yet, I fail so often. I hang my head in shame as I remember that only yesterday I was short-tempered and not the understanding mother my children needed. Thank You for forgiving me, giving me a new day to try again. It seems I stumble and fail so often, but thank You for reaching down in Your mercy and whispering, "I know, dear, and I care. Just take My hand and depend on Me. I see your heart and that's what counts. Together, we will continue our journey of motherhood. Remember, remaining faithful is what counts." Thank You, Father. *Amen.*

◇◇◇◇

Dear Heavenly Father, thank You for speaking so plainly to me through Your Word. It is so easy to grasp those simple facts. And yes, dear Father, as You know, my heart's desire is to be a blessing and not a stumbling block in the life of my husband, my children, and those I meet. May You freely have Your way in my life. *Amen.*

◇◇◇◇

Dear Father in Heaven, Father of Love, Mercy, and Justice: this morning, I praise You for being good. All that You are and do is good. My desire, Lord, is to remain in You, and stay in touch with Your Spirit so that I am not pulling down, but building our house. This morning, I ask that You convict me in any area where I am pulling down and not building. May Your wisdom and light shine forth in our life and home. *Amen.*

◇◇◇◇

Jesus, I can imagine how composed, calm, and serene You were as Judas and his little party came with nothing else in mind but betraying You. You didn't react, but calmly asked, "Whom are you seeking?" As I go about the day, may You remind me from time to time "Whom are you seeking?" and may it make a difference in how I respond to our little ones and to my husband. *Amen.*

◇◇◇◇

Dear Father, I thank You that no matter what we humans experience, there is nothing too painful and distorting for Your healing power to touch and restore. Thank You for the reminder of the little girl I heard about, who suffered innocently at the hands of her parents. I know that the only way our children will hear pleasant voices from our bedroom is if we are walking in Your light in true brokenness, resulting in my husband and me being one. I thank You for Your gift of a marriage where love reigns. And yes, Father, thank You for reminding me who suffers the most when we choose to walk in discord. *Amen.*

⬦⬦⬦⬦

Dear Father in Heaven, I thank You for being my changeless friend. Thank You for giving me Your heart and mind. Thank You for guarding and comforting me. Thank You for rejoicing with me, and thank You also for wiping my tears, and most of all, thank You for showing me Your way. May I in return be all this to my children. I also thank You for my mother, who bears the sweetest name, the one who brought me into this world, the one who cared about me and wanted what was best for me, the one who hurts when I hurt and rejoices when I rejoice. I pray that You would bless her in a special way, and when she passes on, may she rest in the land of her reward. *Amen.*

⬦⬦⬦⬦

Dear Father, Father of Love: I pause this moment to pray for our little family. Again, I recommit each one to You. Our children are yet so small and innocent. May we not neglect our duty of instilling the values of life while they are yet so young and pliable. As they grow up, may they remember our home to be a solid foundation, a home where You were first, a home where they were blessed and protected, a home where they were loved and valued, a home where Mother had time for them in her busy schedule. Father, I pray that You would make that our home and make me that mother. *Amen.*

2
Love, Joy, and Gratitude

Dear Heavenly Father,
thank You that I am now covered and hidden in You because of the blood of Jesus. In order for any other powers to even come close to me, they have to first conquer You. Thank You, God, for making me fearless. Continue daily adorning me with Your whole armor. *Amen.*

◇◇◇◇

Dear Father in Heaven, I thank You for being the great healer. There is nothing too big for You, nothing too frightful or painful that You can't completely heal and set us free from. I've witnessed it with my own eyes, I've experienced it. You've made beauty out of ashes. You've restored my life above what I ever thought would be possible, and the greatest healing and cleansing was when I asked You with all my body, mind, soul, and heart that You would take me to the bottom—that You would take me to the root of my pain, my agony, my turmoil. That is when things started happening. The pain and memories were deep and long, but that's where victory lay. Yes, truly You have touched me like no one else could. *Amen.*

◇◇◇◇

Thank You, Heavenly Father, for giving me that victory, for keeping my heart, for giving me Your peace, and for keeping my mind sound. Such gifts! My heart is humbled to think that in Your greatness, You share Yourself with me. May I be faithful with Your gifts that You bestow upon me. *Amen.*

◇◇◇◇

Thank You, dear Father of Love, Light, Peace, Life, and Truth. Thank You for the blessing of allowing me to live in Your presence. May I be faithful in this span of testing. Thank You that through the blood of Jesus, Your Son, I can dwell in eternity with a new body, living in Your unlimited presence. *Amen.*

◇◇◇◇

Dear Gracious Heavenly Father, I want to take this time to thank You for caring for my heart. For who am I that You think of me? Thank You for being there no matter what part of the day or night I call on You. Thank You for not rejecting me, but nudging me ever onward. *Amen.*

◇◇◇◇

Dear Heavenly Father, thank You for Your healing mercies. Thank You for all the gems I gleaned through the pain, even though it was rough and long. Thank You for choosing me to witness Your transforming power. May those around me see and feel Your power in my daily life, and because of You, may they fear and trust Your unfailing love yet more deeply. *Amen.*

◇◇◇◇

Thank You, Jesus, for officially and by Your authority choosing me to bear fruit. May I be true to Your calling. *Amen.*

❖❖❖

Jesus, because of You, no matter what my day consists of—sick children, being down with the flu, having a day when the children seem to do nothing but fuss, or maybe a day when I have more work than I can squeeze in—because of You, the salvation You brought should be enough to make any day "great." Thank You for coming to this sin-laden earth to die for my sin and free me of the penalty of death. *Amen.*

❖❖❖

Dear Father, I thank You for Your wrath, which does not tolerate sin in my life. I thank You for Your greatness that is so beyond our comprehension. Yet I am thankful for the little glimpses that You reveal of Yourself through Your Word. *Amen.*

❖❖❖

Thank You, dear Heavenly Father, for Your security. Thank You for buying me with a price, and thank You I can now rest in full confidence that, no matter what happens to me, no matter what threatens me, if I'm in Your fold, I'm safe. The enemy can in no way enter that fold, yet he's outside waiting for the minute I venture where You would not go. Thank You for giving me confidence of that security. *Amen.*

◇◇◇◇

Dear Jesus, thank You for taking my place. I was doomed for hell. There was no other way out. Then God sent You to deliver me. They crowned Your head with thorns instead of mine. They spit in Your face instead of mine. You were nailed to the cross instead of me. Thank You. *Amen.*

◇◇◇◇

Dear Heavenly Father, thank You for desiring a close relationship with me, for communing with me, guiding me with Your eye. And having my eyes set on You, I know what You approve of and what is displeasing to You. Thank You for the joy You bring to my heart in knowing You. *Amen.*

◇◇◇◇

Dear Jesus, thank You for being in authority. It's hard for me to grasp Your being able to listen to everyone all at the same time, all the time. I find comfort just being in Your presence because I know I'm safe. There is no power greater than Yours. You are the one who deals justly. Thank You for that protection. *Amen.*

◇◇◇◇

Thank You, Heavenly Father, for all the blessings You've sent into my life. Some losses have seemed so grievous, so long and painful…yet I've found that in Your timing, You've restored me yet richer than I've been before. Thank You for the assurance You give me: because I'm Your child, nothing just happens in my life. Either it's Your perfect will or You allow it. And You redeem each situation, turning it into my good for Your glory. *Amen.*

◇◇◇◇

Dear Gracious Father, thank You for sending Jesus to die on the cross, that through His shed blood I can now enjoy a rich relationship with You. I am humbled that You, my righteous, unsearchable Father, desire to live in me and through me. Show and pour forth Your love, Your patience, and Your kindness to those around me. All I can do is humbly fall on my knees and, with an overwhelming heart of gratefulness, say thank You. *Amen.*

◇◇◇◇

Dear Heavenly Father, I thank You for still being the same faithful Father that You were in Noah's day— that no matter how great the trauma in my life, You are still able to deliver and see me through victoriously. And may You smell a sweet savor from my life as You did from Noah's sacrifice (Genesis 8:21). May I be enfolded in Your love. *Amen.*

◇◇◇◇

Dear Heavenly Father, thank You for being God, for being holy, and for Your being above all. No longer do I quake and tremble in Your presence, but a deep peace has overtaken my soul, knowing You delight in my presence. You delight in having a close relationship with me. I was created by You for Your honor. You made a provision through Jesus' death and resurrection that I no longer stand doomed, but redeemed! Thank You, Father. *Amen.*

◇◇◇◇

Thank You, Heavenly Father, for putting me in the position of lacking nothing. Thank You for the shelter of Your wing and the protection of my husband's wing. Thank You also for the shelter the body of Christ provides for my family and me. Thank You for Your goodness, Your love, Your forgiveness, Your redemption, and Your protection. Yes, in You, I truly lack nothing. *Amen.*

◇◇◇◇

Thank You, dear Father, Creator of Heaven and Earth. Thank You for You being so glorious above what I can grasp, and yet providing a mediator, that through Jesus I could be reconciled to You. And now as a frail human, I get to enjoy the benefits of being Your child, of sharing Your kingdom, of tasting Your goodness. Thank You for Your act of love on my behalf in sacrificing Your only Son for my sake. *Amen.*

◇◇◇◇

Dear Father, thank You for being my rock, my all, my sure foundation, my ever-comfort. May I be sensitive to those around me, looking on the heart as You do. And thank You for the experience in my life of being misunderstood. Thank You for the peace You have given me as I've rested in You, my sure, unchangeable foundation. You never misjudge my motives, but see my heart as it is and convict me of things displeasing to You. Thank You for being faithful. *Amen.*

◇◇◇◇

Dear Faithful Father in Heaven, thank You for salvaging me, not because of what I did, but because of Your great love. You stooped and took my hand and rescued me. You didn't stop there, but You exchanged my filthy, muddied, and decayed cloth for Your heavenly robe and set me in Your kingdom to labor faithfully till death. May I, like Simeon, who blessed the infant Jesus, remain in this state, so that I can pass on in peace. *Amen.*

◇◇◇◇

Dear Jesus, thank You for Your act of love. You endured all that You passed through on earth so I could become Your sister, so that I could be saved from eternal doom. And You didn't stop there. I get to inherit Your whole kingdom. And now, why do I forget to daily overflow with praise in my heart? Your love is so unfathomable. May I reflect that love to my husband, my children, and those around me. Thank You, Jesus. *Amen.*

◇◇◇◇

Dear Father, thank You for Jesus. Truly, as Simeon told Joseph and Mary, because of this Jesus, some will fall, some will rise, all hearts will be revealed. Thank You for sending Him to release me from my captivity, from my slavery, and setting me free and bringing about healing in my life. Today, the calves that were turned loose went with a spring in their steps. Truly, I can identify with them. *Amen.*

◇◇◇◇

Dear Jesus, thank You for bearing my pain, my shame, my condemnation, my guilt, and my grief. Thank You for not being someone who only *tries* with the best of His ability to identify with our grief. No, You know perfectly. There's nothing too deep for You, nothing too painful…Thank You for Your comfort, Your assurance, Your urging me onward. I'm looking forward to the time that I will get to meet You face-to-face. Until then, I thank You for being there for me, for being my all. *Amen.*

◇◇◇◇

Dear Loving Father in Heaven, thank You for Your protection, for Your shield of faith, for Your breastplate of righteousness. Thank You for Your peace and Your truth. Thank You for Your whole armor, wherewith I stand in complete protection. No longer do things just happen to me. Really, there are no accidents in my life. Either it's Your perfect will or You allow it for my good. The devil and his workers have lots of power and are ever so corrupt. Yet, You are all powerful. No power ever was, or will be, greater than You. Thank You for that security. *Amen.*

◇◇◇◇

Dear loving Father, this morning I want to thank You for the Father You are to me, for being my best friend. Thank You for Your gentleness. When I'm sad, You are always there. When I need to talk, You always listen. When I need comfort, I can feel Your gentle touch. When I grieve broken friendships, You remind me that Your relationship with me will never be severed. Thank You for letting me rest in Your arms when I grow weary, and thank You for ever urging me onward. Because of You, life is worth living. Because of You, it will be worth dying. *Amen.*

◇◇◇◇

Dear Father, You are so unsearchable, so unfathomable, so past finding out. My power is no power compared to Yours. The more I get to know You, the more I want to know about You. Thank You that Your Word is nourishing and new every morning, every hour, every moment. And thank You for giving us free rein to Your Word. The strength it gives is never limited. My desire is to become more and more like You and someday exchange my physical body for a heavenly one, where I can be in Your unlimited presence. *Amen.*

◇◇◇◇

Good morning, Father. Thank You for another day, a gift from You. This is a morning that I simply don't feel like…But thank You, Father, for reminding me that feelings are just that—feelings. They are neither right nor wrong. Now that I've chosen to sing despite my feelings, my heart is already uplifted. I am looking forward to another day with words of praise on my lips. For truly, having a Father whose understanding and power are infinite is enough to cheer me on, on *any* day. *Amen.*

◇◇◇◇

Thank You, Father in Heaven, for being my strong tower and my strong rock. I'm hidden in You, and there I know I'll be safe because there is nothing stronger than You. So really, Father, there's nothing that I face in life that needs to strike fear. You are my master, my ruler, my conqueror—You are my all. In You, I sweetly rest. *Amen.*

◇◇◇◇

Dear Everlasting Father, I praise You for being just that—everlasting. Truly, I've never been disappointed or let down when I have sought Your face. And I'm being fulfilled daily. Life is no longer something to endure, but a pleasure. Each day, as I rise, I remember You as my Father and I remember my purpose-filled life, and again I press toward the goal of my high calling. Thank You for being there for me when I knock, seek, and ask. *Amen.*

◇◇◇◇

Dear Father in Heaven, thank You for giving me sweet rest. As I kneel each morning and give the new day into Your hands, I feel so free, so light. As I go about my day knowing that You will fight, I rest—all I need to do is work and trust. I know that being at rest in You is one of the greatest gifts I can offer my children. *Amen.*

◇◇◇◇

Lord, Father of All, thank You for the broadening experience that has come from our traveling through Your creation. I also take this opportunity to thank You for our godly heritage. May we be diligent in doing what it takes to pass it on. *Amen.*

◇◇◇◇

Lord Jesus, thank You for the perfect example You are to me in letting pain make You and not break You. You were without fault, yet You learned obedience through the things You suffered. Thank You for all the pain You led me through. My past was rugged, heart-rending, and cruel. The valley was deep and seemingly endless, and yet I thank You for the path You chose for me. It has done something to me that I would never exchange. Your transforming power that I witnessed in my own life is a special gift from You that I cherish. Dear Jesus, You see the pockets of pain that I still hit at times. I praise You that I no longer despair or ask You to take it away, but trust that You would lead me safely right through it to Your healing power. It causes me to once more cast my all in Your care, realizing how weak and frail I am of my own, and how useless it is to try life on my own. My gratefulness cannot find the proper words to express what I feel. May my life show that I have learned obedience by the things I suffered. *Amen.*

<><><>

Dear Father in Heaven, thank You for Your protection on that day I can't forget, so many years ago. You had more pleasure in my life than in my death. And as I ponder the years since then, I thank You for the restoring, renewing, and reforming You have done in my life. My life is richer and fuller than ever before.

But what's more, I thank You for rescuing me from eternal doom, for sending Jesus, who was willing to make the sacrifice so that I can now look forward to spending eternal life with You. *Amen.*

◇◇◇◇

Dear Father of Love and Justice, thank You for extending the invitation to me. "Come," You said, "all things are ready now." Thank You for the great sacrifice You made in preparing the feast, in taking upon Yourself all my sin, all my shame and guilt. Because of me, You suffered and gave Your own life that I can live. Would I pay the price it takes to accept? Yes, Jesus, the price is great—no longer on my own, no longer fulfilling my desires, my dreams, and my hopes, but Yours. It isn't without pain and suffering, but the joy far outweighs the pain and I would never choose to turn back. We have also, as guests, taken a piece of ground, and I have also taken a husband. May those riches and possessions never overpower my desire for You. Thank You again, Jesus, for Your invitation. Only through You can I remain faithful. *Amen.*

◇◇◇◇

Dear Father in Heaven, thank You for being a true example for us in lavishing Your love on Jesus, and that now Jesus has fulfilled Your plan in dying the death of a sinner, yet without sin—He died that I can live. The pain You suffered, the sacrifice You made, the price You paid to set me free—in that very act You were telling me, "Daughter, I love you and I care about you." My desire is to freely pass that love on to my family and all I meet. *Amen.*

◇◇◇◇

Father of Love and Mercy, thank You for the security it brings to my life to know You are the builder of my house. There is no one, nothing, that can build a stronger one. That means I have a sure foundation so when storms hit I don't need to be shaken, fearful, or moved. Thank You for all You have done for me in resurrecting me from a tattered, worn building to one with a sturdy foundation. May the warmth and light of You in my heart continue shining through to those around me. *Amen.*

◇◇◇◇

Father in Heaven, I thank You for the lesson You have taught me. Mistakes, flops, and failures for me are no longer devastating since I am reminded each time that I have the opportunity to try again. Thank You for always forgiving and helping me up and onward. With You at the lead, we can conquer anything. I find our journey a joy. I never know what will be around the next curve, but with You, I can do all things (Philippians 4:13). *Amen.*

◇◇◇◇

Dear Father of Love and Justice: as I grow deeper into Your love, I find myself developing a deeper gratefulness to You because of Your anger toward sin, and a deeper gratefulness for Your forgiveness when I sin. May I be diligent in heeding Your words, remembering Lot's wife, and not looking back. My desire is to serve You with my whole heart, keep Your precepts, and have Your Word hidden deep within my heart at all times. *Amen.*

◇◇◇◇

Dear Father in Heaven, thank You for being God. Thank You for the security it brings to me in knowing You have power over all powers. You are the one in ultimate authority. This morning, I also pause to thank You for all the barren times in my life. Many times, I turned to You with groaning from deep within and You heard even if there were no words. The pain made me turn to You and seek You with all my heart. I realized if there's nothing more to life than pain, then life wouldn't be worth living. Finding You was finding life! And yes, life abundantly. *Amen.*

◇◇◇◇

Dear Jesus, thank You for being the mediator between God and man. You gave up the bliss of Heaven and came to earth to show us the way. You didn't come and *tell* us the way—You came and walked with us and showed us by example. You met much pain and sorrow and feeling overwhelmed as You labored for Your Father and paved a highway for us. There is nothing we meet up with that You haven't experienced. I thank You for that gift of knowing You feel with us and are always ready to comfort. *Amen.*

◇◇◇◇

Dear Father in Heaven: this morning, I bask in Your love. You are my Father and I am Your daughter. With You I feel safe. I feel loved and wanted. You created me for Your glory. My desire, Father, is to never let You down. May I be lost in You so as not to interfere with the heavenly work that You have called me to. This morning, I feel like I am lacking nothing. You have bought me with a price and now I am loved, cherished, well taken care of. What's more, I belong. You are my Father and that's sufficient. *Amen.*

◇◇◇◇

Father in Heaven, the giver of good gifts: that's where I was, in a pile of filth. And in trying to clean up, I got all the more bemired in the filth of this world. You heard my cry and reached out and lifted me up. Up out of the filth, guilt, and shame. You washed me in Your blood. You didn't even try patching, washing, and fixing my old clothes—You did away with them and clothed me with the garment of Your salvation. You covered me with Your robe of righteousness. My heart is lifted in joyful praise as I bask in the new life. The old is gone and all things have become new. Thank You, Father, is all I can say. *Amen.*

⬦⬦⬦⬦

Dear Father, this morning I thank You for my pain. I thank You that it is a reminder to keep looking to You as my all. I thank You also for the abandonment and suffering that I experienced in my life. You had my good in mind—You would have never allowed it if You wouldn't have been able to make me a better person because of it. Yes, truly, I can embrace my past with fondness, knowing You were there. I was loved. I was well taken care of. Thank You, Jesus. *Amen.*

⬦⬦⬦⬦

Father, this moment I pause to praise You for being God. You are able to do exceedingly above what we ask or even imagine (Ephesians 3:20). It makes me smile as I realize that I am the child of such a King, a King who is able, a King who has endless resources, a King who has all power in Heaven and in earth and who will reign forever. It makes me realize that no matter what happens in my life, there is nothing that is great enough to destroy me or take me from Your hand (John 10:29). May I continue to hide in You as You win each battle. *Amen.*

◇◇◇◇

Father, the Mighty Conqueror: thank You for Your protection. I feel so armed, so protected because You are my Father, my warrior. My battles are Your battles. Anyone or anything that assails me is assailing You, and there is no power greater than You, so that means I'm secure. I cherish that word *secure*. In You, I am free from risk of loss, free from danger, free from fear or distrust. May You continue clothing my household and me with Your armor lest we become prey for the enemy. Thank You, Father, for being my mighty conqueror. *Amen.*

◇◇◇◇

Dear Father, I thank You for my birthday because it means that I was born. Thank You for creating me in Your image, for making every detail of me just the way You did. Truly, I am fearfully and wonderfully made. Thank You for the way You have cared for me through all that I have faced. It gives me the confidence that nothing will ever happen to me the rest of my life that You are not able to see me through. Thank You for rescuing, redeeming, restoring, and renewing me. Thank

You for being *for* me—it makes all the difference in my life. I also thank You for choosing my father and mother to be my parents. As I keep pondering the past years, I sit here in awe, and words don't seem to work in trying to express my thankfulness to You, God, for Your wonderful work in my life. Thank You. *Amen.*

◇◇◇◇

Dear Jesus, I am sure I will never know the depths of Your struggle and agony that night in the Garden of Gethsemane. But I do know that it was a victorious struggle and that it was because of me. You saw my lost state, and unless You went through the struggle, bearing my sin, my guilt, and my shame, I would remain just that—*lost*. Yes, eternally doomed. As I sit here wondering what words to use to tell You how much I appreciate what You have done for me, what You are doing for me, and what You will do for me, I just don't find any words that work. It is something that goes beyond understanding. My desire is that my life be wholly lost in You, so that others might see You through me and glorify Your name. *Amen.*

⬦⬦⬦⬦

Dear Father, thank You for Your redemption, because of which I have no need to wallow in self, thinking of myself too highly or too lowly. But in You, I am no longer condemned. For there is therefore now no condemnation to those who are in Christ Jesus (Romans 8:1). In You, I am deeply loved. In You, I am completely forgiven. In You, I am fully pleasing. In You, I am totally accepted. In You, I am complete. Thank You, Father, for sending Jesus, who was willing to give His life and rise victoriously so that I am now a new creation of immeasurable worth. Thank You. *Amen.*

⬦⬦⬦⬦

Dear Father, Father of Love and Mercy: I thank You for caring and providing for me in a special way. You saw my lost state and sent Jesus to die in my stead. You saved me from eternal doom. If You cared about my lost state so much that You gave Your only Son, then I know You are a Father worth having, trusting, and believing. I also thank You for the promise that whatever work You have called me to do, You will do it in me to completion. It's about remaining in You and trusting You to do Your work through me that counts. Thank You, Father, for caring about every little detail of my life. *Amen.*

◇◇◇◇

Dear Father, thank You for being there for me and listening when I need to talk. I also thank You for Your patience and long-suffering, and forgiving me and giving me another opportunity to do better today than the day before. Without You, life is defeating. It's only through You and in You where victory lies. May You continue urging me onward and upward. *Amen.*

◇◇◇◇

Dear Father in Heaven, this morning I am awed at Your love toward me. You don't want to hold any of Your blessings back. You want to give freely. It's just that too often I forget to ask and believe. You long to open Your windows and pour out Your love, joy, and peace in our hearts and home. May we be in such a state to freely receive, looking to You for our all, having You first in our lives, and making our needs known. Father, thank You for convicting me where I have been failing as a mother to love my children as You love me. Thank You for taking me in Your arms and forgiving me and for giving me the opportunity to start anew. In You, Father, I will continue. *Amen.*

◇◇◇◇

Dear Father in Heaven, I thank You for Your words of comfort to fit each need. I thank You that You never tire of listening to my fears and worries. I thank You that as I settle down for another night, I have the comfort of knowing that You will be awake all night. You will be there whenever we need You, and as I sleep, You are at work refreshing, renewing, and invigorating my body to face another day. I thank You for making me to dwell in safety. *Amen.*

◇◇◇◇

Dear Father of High Calling: I thank You for the great work You have called me to do, training and nurturing Your little angels You have placed in my care. You have called me to bring them forth as shining vessels for Your kingdom. May You continue to press the burden on my heart of the importance of walking in Your ways and of heeding Your commands, lest Your little ones be marred. I also thank You for the joy I find in daily telling our little ones stories of the Bible, applying them to everyday life, and learning with the children new Bible verses every week. My heart overflows as I witness them grasping new facts about You and new aspects of You, our living God. *Amen.*

◇◇◇◇

Dear Father, many years ago, You sent Your Son, Jesus, to this earth to walk with us, to love us and show us the way, dying on the cross for the redemption of the world. Now, years and years later, we still set aside a day as a remembrance of the day that Jesus was crucified. I know that even though the event happened long ago, it still has the same effect on us believers as if it had happened yesterday. The story will never grow old. For all things have become new, old things have passed away. *Amen.*

◇◇◇◇

Father, not only do I want to celebrate today, but may my life show by the fruits of the Spirit that I am celebrating every day the deliverance that Jesus brought to my soul. *Amen.*

◇◇◇◇

Dear Father in Heaven: at this moment, I pause to thank You for how uniquely You have created me as a woman. You placed within me all the organs necessary to grow and give birth to our little babies. I thank You for creating me to be a helpmeet for my husband. I thank You for making me. May I out of that thankfulness and gratitude to You, pass on to our little ones how delightful they are in simply being who God created them to be, boys and girls, men and women. *Amen.*

◇◇◇◇

Dear Father in Heaven, my heart is touched as I reflect on Your Son's response to the criminal who was being crucified at His side. Jesus, You were in deep pain and agony, carrying the load of my sins and the sins of the whole world. Yet You heard the faint whisper of the man at Your side. He repented in the last hour and You took him in. That's You—You're near and You hear. And You remember me no matter where I am or what I face. *Amen.*

◇◇◇◇

Dear Father, thank You for always being there. I find it such a joy in teaching our children about You. You put our souls to rest knowing that You are in control of every situation and that Your power far exceeds any other power. Thank You for the gift of prayer whereby we have access to You continually. *Amen.*

◇◇◇◇

Dear Father, thank You for being You, and thank You for all the things You have sent into my life, especially the pain of my past. It didn't make sense why You chose this path for me, yet now as Jesus is being glorified in it, I thank You from the depth of my heart for this experience. You have taught me that Your power of healing far exceeded the greatest trauma of life and that through You, it is possible to embrace each situation, thanking You for the richness it has brought into my life. It is with fondness that I remember all the acts of love You have done for me, even before I was born. *Amen.*

◇◇◇◇

Dear Father in Heaven, I praise You for being God, for being flawless and good. I thank You for fulfilling me and for giving me what You see fit. Thank You for teaching me that when my love for You is greater than my earthly desires, I am content. Thank You for fulfilling my deepest need—and that need is for You. Without You I am as a sheep gone astray, lost and crippled. But You sent Jesus to rescue, salvage, and redeem me. Thank You, Father! *Amen.*

◇◇◇◇

Dear Loving Father, thank You for the inspiration that the life of Hannah, the mother of Samuel, has been to me. She was faithful and true to You year after year, even though she wasn't granted her request for a long time. Whether with a son or without one, she was dedicated to You, and therefore she was able to be faithful when You did give her her desires. As You blessed Hannah with her request, so have You blessed me over and over. You have placed in our care two precious souls, You have blessed me with a loving husband. Keep reminding me that all these treasures are Yours. And only as I remain faithful will You keep entrusting me with more responsibilities. *Amen.*

◇◇◇◇

Dear Father, thank You for keeping from me the full beauty of Heaven. I know if I should comprehend it here on earth, I would never be able to enjoy life in this rusty cage. Thank You for all the earth and its beauty, which You have designed for my pleasure. May I never feel guilty to enjoy it as You have intended. But I do look forward to the time when You will call me onward. May I be prepared to leave joyfully at any given moment. *Amen.*

3

Friendship and Fellowship

Christ Jesus,
here I am, here's my heart. It's Yours, Yours to do with as You see fit. Use me, shape me, mold me so that I in return can give my whole heart to my husband and to my brothers and sisters around me. Thank You for the freedom and the richness it brings. *Amen.*

◇◇◇◇

Dear Heavenly Father, You know my desire to be lost in You, which results in being lost in the body of believers, which results in being a part of the express image of You. Such a weighty work You have called me to fulfill. May I be found faithful. And convict me of anything that could be or is a hindrance in my portraying the express image of You. *Amen.*

◇◇◇◇

Jesus, thank You for setting such an example for me. There must not have been a touch of self anywhere near Your heart as You stooped to wash Judas's feet.

May that love and compassion be mine as I mingle with my brothers and sisters in the church and for each soul I meet; and may it be that I could at any moment stoop with a heart that reflects Yours while washing my sisters' feet. *Amen.*

◇◇◇◇

Dear Jesus, thank You for Your example of unselfishness, for remembering me just moments before Your hour of betrayal was at hand. May I follow Your example in remembering the heartaches and trials in the lives around me, and have a true godly concern for their souls instead of dwelling on the pain that goes with my own testings. *Amen.*

◇◇◇◇

Dear Heavenly Father, thank You for the example the older women in our congregation are to me. Truly, as set off by their modest dress, their meek and gentle ways are the result of Your adorning. May I follow their example and be lost in You by daily taking time to read and meditate and commune with You. May those around me see my life decorated, beautiful, and garnished with Your character. *Amen.*

◇◇◇◇

Dear Father in Heaven, I know You intend that brethren live together in peace. May I take the second mile in my relationship to the women of our congregation. I have experienced that mistrust, imaginations, and false assumptions are a sure destroyer of relationships. May I truly be free of such, that Philippians 4:8 would be a part of my very being; that I could think of my sisters with thoughts of honesty and purity, with thoughts of things that are just, lovely, and of a good report. *Amen.*

◇◇◇◇

Dear Father in Heaven, Father of Mercy and Truth: may I never be lax in bringing our hurting family, friends, and loved ones to You. You are well able to restore and heal. Some seem so weary, almost too weary to find the way to Your side. Others have lost their desire, while others are blinded by sin, and still others are bound and controlled by childhood traumas. May I never be the cause of any of these stumbling further, but may they see something in my life that draws them to You. *Amen.*

◇◇◇◇

Dear Father in Heaven, I know that You are still looking for and using those who will bridge the gap. I realize that's a part of being in Your kingdom. Maybe it is just laying a hand on the shoulder of a struggling friend; maybe it's praying for the needs of someone You know; maybe it's peacemaking between squabbling children; maybe it's in approaching someone who is in error. Maybe it's in bridging the gap between God and man simply by the life I live. The list could go on and on. Father, here I am, a vessel—use me. May I be found worthy of Your calling in bridging the gap. *Amen.*

◇◇◇◇

Dear Father in Heaven, I thank You for my friend and the inspiration she is to me. Yes, she is taking a step before us. It almost makes me lonely that she gets to move on and receive life in full, and I am kept to linger on. Father, I do long to be with You in the heavenly awe and bliss that's too great for our earthly bodies to bear. Yet, if I think of my husband and children, I can identify with the apostle Paul as he wrote, "I am hard-pressed between the two, having a desire to depart and be with Christ, which is far better. Nevertheless to remain in the flesh is more needful for you" (Philippians 1:23-24). Yet, if I pass on, I want it to be a joyful occasion, a celebration. Yes, my loved ones can grieve and mourn, but may it last for only a moment as they remember that precious in Your sight is the death of Your saints. *Amen.*

◇◇◇◇

Dear Father of Heaven and Earth, thank You for so clearly and plainly having Your Word and will written to us, where we can learn from the lives of others. May my life be a sincere life; may my prayers, my sacrifices, wearing plain garments, and going to church be a result of having You in my heart; may all of these be an outward sign of an inward change. Yes, my sins were crimson, they were scarlet, but You washed them white as snow with Your blood. *Amen.*

◇◇◇◇

Dear Father in Heaven, it is with a repentant heart that I come before You. I was entertaining not-so-nice thoughts about my friend. I was priding myself that I was not wallowing in self-centeredness as she was. Lord, forgive me, for I have failed. May I use this as a reminder to never judge my sister. For often I only see in part. The picture I form is often so incomplete. May I extend trust to others as I would like them to trust me. *Amen.*

◇◇◇◇

Thank You, Loving Father, for the encouragement and inspiration the older experienced mothers are to us young mothers who are in the harness of mother-hood. To witness them come through victorious and see their children walk in truth is a great comfort. May I follow their example of momently coming to You to be refreshed and reinvigorated. *Amen.*

◇◇◇◇

Dear Everlasting Father, thank You for reminding me how temporary and fleeting things of this world are. May I be diligent in storing up heavenly treasures: friendships, spending time with my children, being there for my husband, praying for the lost and dying, supporting the ministry. Thank You also for blessing me with sharing and caring brothers and sisters through times of earthly loss. Make me sensitive to the needs around me. *Amen.*

◇◇◇◇

Dear Eternal Father of Heaven and Earth: I thank You for the gift of loving brothers and sisters who we can gather with every Sunday to talk and learn of You. Thank You for the gift of the Bible. Its contents are full of life and hope. This morning, I also pray for the ministry. May You bless them for their faithfulness in preparing week after week to feed us of the living bread. May You strengthen them and give them courage to do their all in what You have called them to, so that they deal justly with their flock. May we as a family make their calling a joy and not a burden. *Amen.*

◇◇◇◇

Dear Father of Life, thank You for being God. Thank You for having power over all powers. Your ways, which are "past finding out" (Romans 11:33), are such a comfort to me as we near the parting of our dear sister in Christ and friend. You are in charge, You are in control, and Your timing is perfect. To You a thousand years are only as a day. In light of eternity, it will only be a day and then our sorrow will be past, then judgment. Thank You for the gift of Your Spirit in making it possible to remain faithful to the end. *Amen.*

◇◇◇◇

Lord, condition my heart that I would recognize Your angels, Your servants, and Your children. They might need only a smile to urge them onward, a pat on the shoulder, a listening ear, or a helping hand that could make a difference in their journey out of Sodom. Lord, make me sensitive to the needs around me. *Amen.*

◇◇◇◇

Dear Father, thank You for being good. When I see the pain around me, people suffering innocently, I wonder, *Why, Lord?* Yet I believe You are a good, just God and all You send—pain and sorrow and joy—is all for our good, in molding and shaping us for Your eternal good. Thank You for the examples of those around as they suffer in sorrow. The burning love and faithfulness they show their families even during betrayal. It is heart-moving. The joy they have in living, despite pain and broken dreams, speaks volumes. May You bless them in a special way and enfold them in Your arms of love as they gather strength for each new day. *Amen.*

◇◇◇◇

Dear Father, thank You for the many gifts You bestow upon us daily. Thank You for the gift of our brotherhood, who work together in unison, which results in strong Christian homes, which results in an effective, up-building school. I also thank You for each of those forty-three pupils who put their effort in to make the program a success. May You bless each one of them in a special way. I also pray for the fathers and mothers of all those children. May You bless each one of them for the many little things they do in bringing up their children in Your ways. May we remain faithful in the many little things that we are called to do in Your kingdom. *Amen.*

◇◇◇◇

Dear Father, I thank You for being Father and Lord of all. I thank You that Your salvation doesn't depend on degrees, diplomas, and education, but that it is designed so everyone, no matter who he is, is able to come into Your fold by believing on Your Son and depending on Your righteousness. This morning, I also pray for the man we met the other day. May a little flicker of light be kindled. May he come to realize that nothing is able to make us good enough to enter into eternal rest but the Father's righteousness alone. *Amen.*

◇◇◇◇

Dear Father of Love, I'm awed at the weighty work that You have called me to do. You are depending on me to bring up godly men, and You are looking to me to be my husband's hidden strength. God, without You I fail, without You I stumble and fall. I cannot, God. But You can, and I will let You. Today, convict me and move me to be a mother and wife who makes a difference in the world of faithful men. *Amen.*

◇◇◇◇

Good morning, Father. This is a special morning to me. Today I again anticipate gathering with our local body of believers, and truly from my heart, I can echo the words, "How good and how pleasant for brethren to dwell together in unity!" (Psalm 133:1). It's a day that we gather with prepared hearts and anticipate a prepared sermon. This morning, I also pray for each of the members in this body of Christ. May each of us have a zeal for You, motivating us to good works. May all of us bask daily and deeply in Your Word and in Your love. And may we not be found doubting, but believing each word You have said to be true. Thank You, Father, for this wonderful gift of belonging to Your body. *Amen.*

◇◇◇◇

Dear Father, at this moment I pause to pray for our struggling friend and the workload of caring for her special-needs daughter and all that goes with it. May You also bless all my sisters who have reached out in love and compassion and showed their concern not only in words but in action. That is the desire of all of us sisters—to be true vessels in Your vineyard. Thank You, Father, for my sisters in You who are walking in Your Spirit and ways. *Amen.*

◇◇◇◇

Dear Father, tears well up in my eyes as I think of the little one who's gone before us, so sweet, innocent, and pure. He came and then he left, a little angel with a message for me. My heart burns with a desire to be where he is now, in Heaven at Your side where there is no pain, no tears, only peace and joy forevermore. This morning, my heart goes out to his parents as they grieve the loss of their little dreamed-for son. May Your arms of love be a comfort for their hurting souls, and may they find comfort in knowing they didn't lose their son. For nothing is ever lost if You know where it is. May his father and mother take courage to remain faithful until You call them home to where their little son is. Thank You again, Father, for sending this little boy with his message to touch my heart and many others. *Amen.*

◇◇◇◇

Dear Heavenly Father, I thank You for the many friendships I share. First of all, for my husband, my parents, my brothers and sisters-in-law, sisters in the church, aunts, cousins, and friends. I cherish each of these friendships in a special way. May I always be true to You in following Your new commandment that I love everyone as You loved me (John 13:34). And really, Father, You tell me that this is how You and those around me know if I am Your disciple. You take great notice of how I relate to, respond to, and interact with others. *Amen.*

◇◇◇◇

Thank You, Father, for Your many blessings. My heart is overflowing with gratefulness for my many sisters in Christ who are walking with me the same path of the daily ups and downs and challenges of motherhood. I find it a great blessing walking together and sharing tips, ideas, and what works most effectively for them. Thank You, also, Father, for Your promise of giving wisdom to those who ask. *Amen.*

◇◇◇◇

Dear Father, thank You for the many examples of dedicated women with godly character. Their lives show that they are looking for a reward beyond this momentary life. That is my desire, Father: to be more concerned about what You think of my everyday choices than what men think. May You bless each one of these godly women for the examples they are to me, and truly, may they receive their reward. *Amen.*

◇◇◇◇

Dear Father, at this moment, I pause to thank You for our kind neighbors. Thank You for choosing them to live in the house next door. May You bless them richly for the good example they've been and for giving of themselves to us. May we in return be those neighbors who are always sharing, loving, considering, and respecting. Should our path ever part because of kingdom work, I pray that no matter what the distance, may we always be neighbors in heart. *Amen.*

◇◇◇◇

Dear Father, thank You for Your many wonderful promises and for revealing them to me just when I need them the most. Thank You that when we meet up with trials, as has my friend, that we have something deeper than ourselves to turn to for comfort, protection, and peace. Your beauty is so beyond our comprehension—the more I grasp of it, the more I realize how little I have yet discovered. I again place my friend in Your care, trusting that even though we don't understand all the details, You do, and that's enough. Today, Father, I will continue to dwell in Your house. *Amen.*

4

Training the Heart

Thank You, God,

for every trial You have put in my life. Some were hard and rough and the end seemed nowhere in sight. Through every testing, I find myself growing stronger. And through all the testings, I've come to know You in a deeper way. *Amen.*

◇◇◇◇

Dear Faithful Father, thank You for these quiet, special moments when all seems at rest. But thank You, also, for all the rough times You send, reminding me that I am only a pilgrim and stranger passing through on my way to our real home—Heaven. *Amen.*

◇◇◇◇

Jesus, thank You for suffering for me, for bearing all my sin and shame and rejection and then setting me free. Thank You, also, for being there for me when I went through the healing of a deep wound. When every joint and muscle was edged with sharpness of

emotional pain and it hurt to move. Thank You for
healing and taking away the agony, and thank You
also for the experience, which gave me a tiny glimpse
of what You must have suffered. *Amen.*

⋄⋄⋄⋄

Dear Jesus, thank You for making me ordinary. But
thank You for Your adorning in my life. May it be evi-
dent to those around me that You live within. May
they feel Your touch, Your love, and Your gentleness.
Amen.

⋄⋄⋄⋄

Lord, I don't even want to imagine what my children
would experience if I would neglect my duties for one
week. The result would be chaos. Is that the condition
my heart would be in if I would discontinue praising
Your name continually? As I go about my day, may I
not be found slack in recognizing Your goodness, Your
forgiveness, Your long-suffering, Your gentleness, and
Your consistency. *Amen.*

◇◇◇◇

Lord, as I go about the day, remind me how vain it is to fight on my own, how defeating my own attempts are. May I be moved to pause and behold the light of Your countenance and rest in Your arms and whisper, "Fight, God, fight." *Amen.*

◇◇◇◇

Dear Father, remind me when I pray and nothing seems to happen that You lingered yet two days when You heard that Lazarus was sick. And really, Lord, it was because You loved Your friends dearly. May I never question Your timing but know that You are using every stitch of experience to the intent that we may believe. *Amen.*

◇◇◇◇

Jesus, thank You for caring about every detail of my life. Thank You for prompting me to really search out what was troubling me. May I remember that finding my sufficiency in things, or people—anything outside You—is vain. *Amen.*

◇◇◇◇

Dear Father, thank You for sending Your dear Son down from heavenly bliss to this sin-laden earth to die the cruel death of a sinner for my sake—that I could be taken from the death row and promised eternal life. And now, Lord, how could I continue to demand payment from one who offends me? Thank You for setting me free. I choose to follow Your example. *Amen.*

◇◇◇◇

Dear Father of Mercies, thank You for the example of Joseph. His distress was severe and it caused him continual suffering, yet he was faithful. I hang my head in shame as I remember how hurt I've been when something was only a misunderstanding, or when someone was kindly trying to help me and I picked it up as rejection. Thank You, God, for forgiving me. Next time I'm tempted to pick up an offense, remind me of the faithfulness of Joseph. *Amen.*

◇◇◇◇

Dear Heavenly Father, thank You for reminding me what happens if I forget Your mercies, Your deliverance, and Your greatness. I know I often fail in having a thankful heart, and yet it should be lively in every Christian's life. Are You telling me that praising You shows a humbleness of heart, because seemingly the children of Israel's hearts strayed the minute they forgot Your mercies? *Amen.*

◇◇◇◇

Dear Father in Heaven, thank You for adorning me and my family with the whole armor, that we need not fear destruction as we go about the day and as we lie down to rest at night. May I do as Peter was told to do by Jesus: "Put your sword in the sheath." And may it stay there. *Amen.*

◇◇◇◇

Dear Jesus, I'm sorry for every time I've said, like Peter, "I am not." Thank You for revealing to me that what seems so harmless in my mind could mean denying You. May my life show that I'm not ashamed to be recognized as being with You. *Amen.*

◇◇◇◇

Oh to be nothing, nothing
Only to lie at his feet
A broken and emptied vessel
For the Master's use made meet.

Yes, Lord, that's my desire—my heart longing to daily be emptied of self and filled with You that I might not be found wanting. Thank You for filling me, and may it result in Your life spilling out and splashing on those around me. *Amen.*

⬦⬦⬦⬦

Heavenly Father, thank You for being faithful—faithful in sending afflictions in my life, for humbling, overthrowing, redirecting, and refocusing my life. Send into my life whatever You see fit to keep me strong and close to You and those around me. Thank You for the gifts resulting from afflictions in my life. *Amen.*

⬦⬦⬦⬦

Dear Jesus, thank You for giving me the gift of Your peace. Thank You for not giving peace as the world gives (John 14:27), or giving me something that's close to Your peace, but giving me *Your* peace. May those around me see and feel that peace in my daily life. *Amen.*

⬦⬦⬦⬦

Heavenly Father, thank You for being a just God, a God of wrath. Because of Your Son, Jesus, may I be found without spot or blemish. And may I never be the cause of the body of Christ losing its strength.

Search me, O God, and know me. Try me, and see if there is any wicked way in me, and lead me in the way everlasting. *Amen.*

◇◇◇◇

Dear Jesus, thank You that through Your Spirit, I can witness the prints of the nails in Your hands and the wounds in Your side. Thank You for the freedom those wounds have brought in my life. May those around me be able to witness Your marks on me by the words I say, the places I go, the things I do, the way I conduct my very life. *Amen.*

◇◇◇◇

Dear Heavenly Father, thank You for giving me the privilege to walk with You, and that through Your blood, I can be blameless. And only through studying Scripture (Your Word) can I know Your commandments and ordinances. Help me be diligent in seeking and searching, and may I be found as having a heart after You as I echo Mary: "Let it be to me according to your word." *Amen.*

◇◇◇◇

Dear Heavenly Father, I sigh in shame as I remember how many times I have taken my own way, not waiting on You, not taking time to pray. That battle is always so defeating and hollow. Thank You for designing me that only through You can I be victorious. May I learn to depend on You more fully and remember to sleep in Your tent instead of in my own little tent a ways off. *Amen.*

◇◇◇◇

Dear Heavenly Father, thank You for showing me Your character through the humbleness of the place where You chose Your Son to be born. Thank You for reminding me that being in Your will doesn't always mean comfort, but that even our discomfort has meaning in Your plan. May my life show that same humility, and may I find peace and comfort in being in a lowly state. *Amen.*

◇◇◇◇

Dear Father in Heaven, thank You again for Your Word, where we can glean and learn so many little gems about people with godly character. Mary was not in any way boastful of this little baby of hers, which everyone piled in to see and to admire. May I be lowly and humble in spirit as Mary was. May I quietly fulfill my place as wife and mother, and with a quiet spirit ponder Your goodness in my heart. *Amen.*

◇◇◇◇

Dear Heavenly Father, thank You for the gift of detailed instructions, for making Your plan known to me through Your Word. May I be ever so diligent in studying and making myself familiar with Your instructions, and may I be diligent in applying Your instructions as Noah was, that I may find grace in Your eyes. *Amen.*

◇◇◇◇

Dear Father in Heaven, I thank You for the experience that reminded us how fleeting life is and the importance of being ready. You had more pleasure in our life than in our death, or we would no longer be here and our little son would have been an orphan. But in Your goodness, You saw fit that we remain here on earth yet a while longer. Thank You for Your protection, and may our life continue to be so that at any given moment we can remember with joy that if we pass on, we will get to see You. I'm looking forward to that day! *Amen.*

◇◇◇◇

Dear Jesus, thank You for Your example, for not only telling me how to live, but showing me through so many acts of mercy and lowliness. May my heart be as Yours, the heart of a servant, content to stay in the background, continuing to be zealous even if my deeds go unnoticed. Thank You, Jesus, for Your example. *Amen.*

◇◇◇◇

Dear Father of Mercies, thank You for convicting me that worship has nothing to do with feelings. It is thanking You in trials, trusting You when tempted, surrendering when suffering, loving You when You seem distant, and asking when You seem silent. I pause again to pray for my dear friend. I know You will deliver her in due time. May it come about in Your way and in Your timing. *Amen.*

◇◇◇◇

Dear Father, thank You for the gift of that dream. Without You, I could never look those past traumas squarely in the face and give them to You for healing. Truly, You do love me. Had You saved Yourself from those whip furrows, from those wounds, from that agony, I would have remained captive, enslaved, and dragged down with chains of bondage. Thank You, Jesus, for Your transforming power, and for setting me free. *Amen.*

◇◇◇◇

Dear Father, sometimes I simply get weary. I fail, I stumble. Once again I have failed to be patient with the children. I made some wrong choices and caused my husband unnecessary pain. Thank You for Your faithfulness in once again gathering up the pieces, forgiving me, and giving me courage to move onward in my journey. May I learn from each stumble, and may each step help me to grow stronger and more dependent on You. I know that all that happens to me is for my growth, to draw me closer to You, to make me more like You. And remind me that this work You have begun in me You will perform until the end. It is a journey, it takes a lifetime. Thank You, God. *Amen.*

◇◇◇◇

Dear Jesus, I know You must have been hungry after Your forty-day fast, and surely a loaf of bread would have been desirable, but You stood the test. I imagine after Your fast, You were physically weakened, yet You were victorious through all the testings. You were tempted in every area possible. There's nothing I suffer or am tempted with that You haven't experienced.

You have tasted sin—You have taken all of mine and the whole world's on Yourself, yet You were without sin. Jesus, of myself I am so weak, I fail, I fumble, and I stumble. May I learn to be more dependent on You. May I continually be lost in You, for truly that's where victory lies. *Amen.*

<><><>

Dear Heavenly Father, thank You for this dry, hollow feeling that brings to my awareness that my priorities are a bit mixed up. I simply can't function properly without having You first—without stopping, pausing, becoming quiet, and drinking deeply from Your Word. I simply feel like I'm going through a dry spell, and it's no one else's fault but mine. I ask for Your forgiveness in neglecting my relationship with You and for the backsliding that results in other areas in my life. Thank You for picking up the pieces and letting me start out anew. Thank You for being my best friend, my companion, my Savior, and my Master. *Amen.*

◇◇◇◇

Dear Jesus, thank You for caring even for the small details in the lives of Your disciples. You must have been weary talking and teaching all day of heavenly things, yet You cared about the earthly work and occupations of Your disciples. Because of You, they caught a hundredfold the number of fish. Thank You for being interested in the little details of my life, and may I turn to You before I have tried all of my own resources. And yet at times, I fail and try on my own before I finally turn to You in desperation. I can hear Your gentle voice saying, "But dear one, you're learning," and I know that's what counts. Thank You, Jesus! *Amen.*

◇◇◇◇

Dear Father in Heaven, the Father of Love and Mercy, the Father of Truth, thank You for again reminding me how important it is to see the hurting and suffering amongst us as You see them. Yet, Your love is far greater. You were willing to *die* for all of them, and for me. You not only stooped to put me on Your donkey, not only did You cleanse my wounds and try to make something good out of the old—You died, You gave Your life that I could be healed, cleansed, and become a new creation. Thank You, Jesus. May that love overflow from my heart and may I, because of You, be a neighbor to those who need me. *Amen.*

◇◇◇◇

Dear Father in Heaven, Father of Life: thank You for being faithful. Thank You for all the teachings in Your Word and for the many parables that You used in teaching Your disciples, and now us. May I never be content to produce fruit that almost looks like the real kind. Instead, may I be a completely new bottle for new wine (You in my heart), and out of me flow Your love, Your mercy, Your truth, Your forgiveness, and Your life. *Amen.*

◇◇◇◇

Dear Faithful Father in Heaven, may I be just that—full of faith. On Sunday, when the minister expounded on *faithful,* I was moved. Truly, that should be a vital part of being a Christian and yes, that's what I desire. I am inspired to be more faithful in teaching our children. I long to be a more faithful wife to my husband, faithful to those around me, ministering to their needs—that I could be known as a person that is just "there." And I pray, dear Father, that I would remain faithful to the end. I know that if I start out faithful but become sidetracked, it will never be remembered by You. But it's in remaining, enduring, and abiding until You call me home. I am looking forward to hearing those words, "Well done, good and faithful servant." *Amen.*

◇◇◇◇

Dear Father in Heaven, may my life show that I'm built and grounded on You, that no matter what happens, I can remain calm and unshaken, knowing that You are in control. And all that happens to me is for my good, for the betterment of my life. Because You love me is why difficulties and trials show up in my life. Thank You, Father, for Your love that You bestow on me daily. And may I be diligent in passing it on to my children. *Amen.*

◇◇◇◇

Thank You, dear Father in Heaven, for being with me through the fire, through the many rivers and waters. Yes, it was rough, but really, I came through stronger, healthier, and more joyful than before. Yes, the fire was hot, but because of You I wasn't burned. The water was deep, but because of You I didn't drown. The rivers were swift, but because of You I wasn't dashed to and fro. This gives me faith and courage to continue onward, and I know that no matter how many trials I meet or how severe they are, You will go with me. You will lead me, and because of You, I will grow stronger yet. Thank You, Father, for being there. *Amen.*

◇◇◇◇

Thank You, Jesus, for seeing me in that helpless state, like the young man, the only son of his mother, whose coffin was being carried through the city gate. You also saw my lost state, and while I was still dead, You died the cruel death to save me. May I be true to Your touch, to Your call, and live a life of denying self, the world, and all its whims. May it result in experiencing eternal life with You. *Amen.*

◇◇◇◇

Dear Father in Heaven, thank You for reminding me of the difference between a woman who is giving her all to You, and a woman who seeks her own…Yes, truly I want to be found and known as a woman who has Your Word hidden in her heart. And may I hear Your words, as Jesus spoke about the woman wiping His feet: "Her sins, which are many, are forgiven, for she loved much" (Luke 7:47). "Your faith has saved you. Go in peace" (verse 50). May it never be said of me that she is haughty, self-seeking; having a stretched-forth neck, walking so as to seek attention. The difference, Father, is You. May I remain faithful. *Amen.*

◇◇◇◇

Dear Jesus, Master of All, thank You for the many times that You have calmed my storm. Whenever I call, You are there. I know You have often patiently waited until I finally called. You longed to take charge at the beginning but in my humanness, I did it my own way too long. As I experience Your calming influence and I'm getting to know You better, it's easier and easier to turn the storm over to You at the beginning. And then really, the waves I see coming don't even have time to turn into storms. When I slip and start fighting on my own, gently remind me that You are waiting to take charge. *Amen.*

◇◇◇◇

Dear Father of Compassion, this morning as I was making my week's plan, I failed to pause and include You in my schedule. Yes, this is my desire for my week, but if You have other plans or interruptions, then I gladly want to see what You have in them for me. And may I in no way neglect the two souls You have entrusted to our care, so that I would have time to stop my work at any moment to discipline, to teach…maybe just hold them and look at a book when they are tired from their play. *Amen.*

◇◇◇◇

Thank You, Father of Heaven, for that message You sent for me… "This is my beloved Son. Hear Him!" It gives me strength and courage. Yes, truly this Jesus who walked the earth with Your people and did many miracles is Your Son! He's not just an unusual prophet who passed by and then was gone. Jesus, Your Son, lives. He's alive in my heart, and that's why I have courage to face each new day, to conquer each trial, to keep on keeping on. And may I truly hear Him. Thank You for all the words of Jesus Himself. Seeing You in part is glorious and joyous. But I'm looking forward to the time when I will see You in full. Until then, may I heed Your words…"Hear Him!" *Amen.*

◇◇◇◇

Dear Father, thank You for being just that, a Father, someone who has infinite understanding. I know that You know my heart, my longings, my bumps and bruises along life's journey. You don't condemn me, but nudge me ever onward. You're always just a prayer away. Just knowing that You're there and that You understand warms my heart and gives me strength and courage to accept the things I cannot change, and the courage to change the things I can. *Amen.*

◇◇◇◇

Dear Jesus, I know that I've too often been found with the "me first" attitude of the disciples. My desire is to have the mind of You and to become as the little child

You called into Your midst. I know that daily the "me first" attitude wants to rise within me. I ask that You reign freely in me and that because of You, my heart can overflow with the fruits of love, joy, peace, long-suffering, faith, and meekness (Galatians 5:22). And I trust that You will convict every time self wants to raise its ugly head. *Amen.*

◇◇◇◇

Dear Father, I'm thinking over Jesus' parable of the Good Samaritan, and I know that I'm not any better than the Levite and the priest who walked by on the other side. How often have I done it myself? Thank You for convicting me, and I trust You will continue doing so and moving me to stoop and pick up my weary, worn neighbors and take them in prayer to You. Or maybe they simply need a touch of love, a word of comfort, or a smile of cheer. May it never be said of me that "she just walked on by." *Amen.*

◇◇◇◇

Father in Heaven, Father of Love: thank You for invit-
ing me to walk with You. Thank You for the joy and
thrill it brings. I never know what I will meet around
the bend, but one thing is sure—if I'm taking Your
route, You will be there. Without trials, hardships,
and testings, my faith doesn't get exercised. I thank
You for every trial You've taken me through. It's been a
long journey, but truly, my faith has become stronger.
I look forward to continue walking with You, being
exercised in faith. *Amen.*

◇◇◇◇

Dear Holy, Just, and Good Father: I thank You for convicting me. Truly, I have been found guilty. How often
I have been more concerned about myself and the pain
I was suffering than what You were trying to accomplish in me through those rough times. I have sinned.
I renew my commitment to You in serving You with
my all and believing You are good, no matter what
happens. Thank You for forgiving me and offering me
Your hope, Your strength, and Your peace. *Amen.*

◇◇◇◇

Dear Mighty God, Everlasting Father, Prince of Peace: thank You for the effect that Your outstretched arm has had on me. So many times in life I have pledged to make things work on my own. I was not consciously thinking that, but my actions spoke loudly. It grieves my heart how it must have grieved You to see me struggle and struggle on my own. Ever so gently and patiently, You stirred my heart and slowly but surely, step by step, I learned that Your way is the only way. The difference is past finding out. May my life portray Your outstretched arm. *Amen.*

◇◇◇◇

Dear Heavenly Father, Lord of all, who created everything in Heaven and on earth for Your glory: You created me in Your image so that You can use me for the furthering of Your kingdom. How vain it is to boast of my accomplishments, for truly, the only good coming from my life is because of me being in Your hand. I am as the boastful, lifeless axe and saw if I keep any honor for myself. Take me, dear Father, and continue making me an instrument useful in Your kingdom in whatever way You see fit. *Amen.*

◇◇◇◇

Dear Father in Heaven: My prayer is that You wouldn't remove painful experiences in my life, but that You could be glorified through each trial, that my children and others could see that my God truly is the living God. And as I pray, may it always be with an open heart. My desire is to never hide any area of my life from You. I have found that nothing in life has ever made me more broken than pain has. May You continue having Your way. *Amen.*

◇◇◇◇

Dear Father of Love, thank You that I don't need to be someone of the kingdom of this world who seeks to make headlines, but that I get to be in Your kingdom. There I find joy working behind the scenes. I thank You for the gift of being called a homemaker, which the world sees as a lowly position. And yet to me it is kingdom work, a heavenly joy of being able to depend on You as my source of direction and all, as I seek to humbly fill the role You have given me. *Amen.*

◇◇◇◇

Dear Father in Heaven: oh, to have the faith of Abraham! Truly, there must have been a deep relationship between You and Abraham or he would have never stood the test. Why, You told him that through Isaac would come forth descendants uncountable—and now You ask him to offer up his only son. May my life reflect the faith of Abraham and his dependence on You, and may I never need to hear the words "you fool," as did the rich man. *Amen.*

◇◇◇◇

Dear Father of Love, Mercy, and Justice: I praise You for the work of Your Son, Jesus, whereby I am brought into Your family. I thank You for being ever present in our home. I know that I don't always recognize Your presence as I should. I know that many times You have hung Your head in sadness as I've lashed out at the children, become impatient, or haven't given You due honor. Thank You for reminding me of the many wrong reasons we can invite You into our homes. My desire is that You will always be an honored part of our household and that our daily lives will show that it's all about You. *Amen.*

◇◇◇◇

Father of Love and Compassion, thank You for again listening to my story. Thank You for Your patience and Your readiness to take me in Your arms and forgive, to once again dress me in Your righteousness. So often I fail and stumble and take my own route, and I don't even recognize anything is amiss until...until I'm in want. Thank You for all the "in want" times You've sent into my life. For it's only then that I again see all my own unrighteousness and long for something better—You! *Amen.*

◇◇◇◇

Dear Father of Light, thank You for providing a way to rescue us from darkness. You suffered, You agonized, yet You stood the test. You gave Your life that we can now walk in light. And if our eye remains single—set on You—then we will walk in the light, but if our focus is on self, we will remain full of darkness. As the blind man received sight, many witnessed Your mighty work and glorified You. May those around me—my husband and children—witness the light in my life, and may we together glorify You. *Amen.*

◇◇◇◇

Lord, Father, thank You for not only telling me as Your child what to do, but for sending Jesus, who showed me how by example. You don't make me guess, but give me clear direction on what is expected of me and what brings peace to my soul. My desire is, Lord, to observe Your ways and follow them as the children follow me. Lord, the work is too weighty for me. Tender souls are involved that need true direction and examples, so I look to You, Lord, for the pouring out of Your Spirit—may the results be fruitful. *Amen.*

◇◇◇◇

Dear Father, thank You for the many examples in the Bible of people who lived Your way, even into their old age, all the way to their death. Thank You also for those examples in my everyday life, grandmothers and grandfathers, who are a rock for all those following in their steps. That's my desire, Father—to grow old pleasantly, having a heart after You. As I grow older, I long to be a mother to everyone, doing things that last through eternity. I know, Father, it all starts today in being willing, obedient, honest, forgiving, and knowing You personally, daily seeking Your face with all my heart. Yes, my longing, Father, is to grow old pleasantly. *Amen.*

◇◇◇◇

Father in Heaven and on Earth: You are still the same God that You were back in Samuel and Saul's time. You haven't changed and You never will. I thank You for that stability. Sin to You is still sin, and it will not go unnoticed. Thank You for sending a deliverer, One who rescued us from our sins, our pride, our wretchedness. Many times, like Saul, I've failed (1 Samuel 13:7-9). I've grown tired of waiting—the stress has gotten the best of me, and I've panicked and taken things into my own hands. Thank You for Your forgiveness, for taking my hand and helping me rise and face the challenges of life anew, this time depending on You to see me through, even if it means, as it should have for Saul, waiting seven more days. *Amen.*

◇◇◇◇

Dear Father, thank You for being my Father, my All—in weariness, in stressful times, as well as on days when all goes well. This morning, I pause to thank You for the gift of communication. Lord, too often I have guessed and assumed, which turned into imaginations, when only a few words could have saved us a lot of pain. Thank You for convicting me this morning and reminding me of what my husband is feeling. May You continue leading us, molding us, and shaping us into Your image. I also thank You for times like these when life gets rough and we get a glimpse of what we really are made of, and see our need in fully falling on You, and saying, "Father, I can't, but You can." *Amen.*

◇◇◇◇

Dear Father of Love, thank You for the promise You have given me that You will not tempt me above what I am able. Thank You also for the example You were to me in resisting temptation. Keep reminding me that being tempted isn't sin—it's only sin when I give in. I also thank You for the exercise in faith I have experienced in being tempted and for the victory You have given me. I know how vain and defeating it is to resist temptation on my own. But with You it is possible. Thank You. *Amen.*

⟡⟡⟡⟡

Jesus, I thank You for the many times You have reached out Your arm of compassion and caught me. I cherish having You guide my conscience. Many times through the day I am convicted. It's You pricking my thoughts lest I make a wrong choice that leads to greater wrongs. Your strong arm is a comfort to me. I trust You will continue guiding me, convicting me of any wrong thoughts, desires, and attitudes. *Amen.*

⟡⟡⟡⟡

Lord, Father, this morning I pause in awe as I study the life of Saul. His life as a king started out with You, yet giving into jealousy led him from one sin to the next, until finally he lashed out not only at those he thought were the problem but also at others who happened to come into his path. Thank You for the

reminder and the many lessons I can learn from this
account. I am thankful that I feel free of any known
sin in my life. Yet, Lord, I recommit my whole life to
You, mind, body, and soul. May You continue guiding me and convicting me, and may I heed the qui-
etest call. *Amen.*

◇◇◇◇

Dear Father, this morning I thank You for the gift of a
sound, healthy mind. Yet I realize it is also the laziest
part of my body. It takes effort to memorize and fill it
with Your thoughts and ways. Yet with You, it is possible to bring into captivity every thought to the obedience of Christ. This morning, I also pause to thank
You for the inspiration our children are to me. How
willing they are to learn, to trust, and to obey. May I
as their mother not let them down by making wrong
choices along the road. May we together continually
be clothed in Your armor, thoroughly equipped for
every good work. *Amen.*

◇◇◇◇

Lord, Father in Heaven: I'm awed by Your greatness and goodness. As You remain faithful to us all Your days, which will be forever, so You are calling me to be faithful in all my days. Being faithful all the time is what brings security, contentment, and a warm glow to our home. *Amen.*

◇◇◇◇

Dear Father, I thank You for being God. I also thank You for the example of the eunuch who was seeking Your face—and though being in a high position, he humbled himself and asked help of a man who was coming that way. You answered, and he was delivered and went rejoicing on his way. Is that not, Father, how You want me to be? If I struggle or have questions, You want me to humble myself and expose myself and ask directions, whether it may be from my husband, a friend, or a sister in the church. Thank You for proving Yourself faithful over and over in my life. It is with confidence and trust that I move forward, knowing You will always answer, in whatever form You choose. *Amen.*

◇◇◇◇

Dear Father in Heaven, thank You for Your work, Your gift of grace. Do I see my need, or do I go about my way thanking You that I don't gossip like a certain sister, mess up like another, or give into temptation like yet another? Does my attitude show compassion for the stumbling and wayward, realizing that if it were not for Your grace, that would be me? Thank You, Father, for sending Jesus to die the cruel death for my sake, taking upon Himself my sin, guilt, and shame, covering me with Your robe of righteousness, and crowning me with Your peace, joy, hope, and love. Thank You that in You I am justified. *Amen.*

◇◇◇◇

Dear Father of Love and Light, thank You for being all-powerful. Thank You for Your many promises that comfort us, give us hope, and urge us onward. You know that as a mother to my children, I long to never let them down, and I long to always keep my promises. But being human, I do fail, and there is always a chance that something could happen and my promise might not be fulfilled. It is never so with You. You never let us down and You are never slack with Your promises. I also find peace in knowing that You cannot lie. May I continue finding a deep peace and holding fast to the profession of my faith without wavering, knowing that You are faithful who promised. *Amen.*

◇◇◇◇

Dear Father, thank You for answering my prayer. This time, You chose to talk to me through my husband. Thank You for that inspiration. I know that You know the thoughts and intents of my heart—You know I long to be pleasing to You and to be Your faithful servant. And really, now that I think of it, weariness is not a sin. It's only a sin if we give in and let it control us. This is another day for me, yet so new and unmarred. May I look to You each moment as I continue my mothering duties. May I put in extra effort to go the second mile as situations arise, and may I instill deep in the hearts of my children what true love is. *Amen.*

◇◇◇◇

Dear Father, sometimes I grow weary. Yes, weary of dying to self. I grow weary of giving, I grow weary of teaching and disciplining. I long for a stress-free life, a life free of suffering. But as I reflect on Your life, Your walk, and Your ways, I realize anew how selfish I am of myself. If You chose that Jesus, Your only Son, the perfect man, would learn obedience through the things He suffered, then why would You use any other method in teaching me obedience and molding me into a vessel that brings honor to Your name? I recommit my life into Your hands. Deliver me from desiring to save myself. Father, not my will, but Yours be done. *Amen.*

◇◇◇◇

Father, I'm sorry, first of all, in not being true to You, in picking up an offense and not forgiving, which in turn hurt my husband. Truly, I have failed Your grace and let a root of bitterness spring up and defile me. You promised Your grace to be sufficient. I could have chosen to give the hurt to You, releasing my husband and talking about what was bothering me. Instead, I robbed us of our joy and precious time together. Father, thank You for forgiving me, picking me up, and letting me try again. *Amen.*

◇◇◇◇

Dear Father, this morning as I bask in Your love, reflecting in Your light, I bow my head in shame. How often do I grieve Your Spirit by wanting to shape my own vessel in the way I want it and resisting the brokenness You want to bring about in my life? Wanting what I want, the way I want it, only makes me miserable, and Your cleansing in my life is of no effect. Why is it, Lord, that self dies so hard? But really, Father, You didn't promise that Your refining would be without pain. So here I am, Father— once again I recommit my life to You. I allow You to do in my life whatever brings the most honor to Your name. *Amen.*

◇◇◇◇

Dear Father, thank You for being good. Thank You for sending Your Son for my redemption. May the fruits of my life show that I am thankful that You spared my life and rescued me from hell. My desire is to be a faithful prayer warrior and intercede for those who come to mind as You lay the urgency on my heart.

May I never be too busy to pause and intercede. And may I realize that intercession does make a difference and, yes, even saves the lives of others. *Amen.*

◇◇◇◇

Dear Loving Heavenly Father, thank You for the experience at the nursing home. Thank You for the reminder that if life continues, I too will someday be in the shoes of these elderly. The life I live today will make a difference in the life I live when I am old. You know my desire to faithfully fulfill my purpose in life—living my life for You, daily crucifying self and being a true helpmeet to my husband and a loving mother to my children. When I am old and gray and my years are spent, may I relish and cherish the many joyful experiences in life. *Amen.*

◇◇◇◇

Dear Almighty Father, the Giver and Taker of Life: thank You for the gift of eternal life and for the joy and comfort in knowing I never need to die. Thank You for the sacrifice You made, suffering in agony, willing to be nailed to the cross, and then dying. Yes, dying in my stead that I can live. My prayer is that You would continue holding me, guiding and directing me so that my faith in You would remain strong unto the end. Because of You, Father, physical death no longer looks scary to me, but a joy. For after all, that's why You put me on earth to begin with. This battlefield is only a test to see if I will live by Your grace and remain faithful unto the end. *Amen.*

◇◇◇◇

Heavenly Father, I marvel while I ponder Your love, Your provision, and Your care of me as I reflect on the many times I have hit a hard spot. In my eyes, all I've been able to see is the mountains on both sides, the Red Sea that is sure to swallow me, and the enemy that is sure to destroy me. To me, there has been no way out, and I've wondered if the being they call God existed. Now as I look back, I see each of those experiences as a blessing, for that's what You were doing, blessing me. You were leading me out of Egypt—the land of bondage and slavery—to the land of freedom. The path You have chosen for me is no longer scary, even though I never know what's around the next bend. I anticipate each step with joy, knowing that the path You chose for me is headed Your direction, and that staying on Your path means nothing will happen to me that has not already passed Your permission. *Amen.*

◇◇◇◇

Dear Father in Heaven, I thank You for Your many promises. You promised that if I remain faithful and draw from the source of true life, then I will not wither but be fruitful and prosper in whatever I do. You know, Father, how I long to be a fruitful mother and wife. Yet so often I fail. I try drawing life from myself. I stumble and fall and my leaf begins to wither because I don't draw from the living waters. Father, I realize that a prosperous life is all about You and not at all about me. Thank You, Father, for being faithful. *Amen.*

◇◇◇◇

Father of Love and Compassion: thank You for each valley I walk through. I believe that each thorn, each wave, each hill, each trial that You send my way is because You love me and desire to keep reforming and transforming me more and more into Your likeness. And really, Father, I know that it's through the valleys that I grow the most. May Your will be done. *Amen.*

<><><>

Dear Father, thank You for the trials that motherhood brings. At the time, it doesn't feel good and I wish to escape for a moment and capture some time for just myself. But, Father, I realize if motherhood were all roses, we would never learn the priceless gift of always leaning on You and realizing that all good gifts come from You. Remind me today to choose to be joyful, no matter what the circumstances are that I'm facing. Thank You, Father, for sending me enough roses to urge me onward and enough thorns to keep me humble. *Amen.*

<><><>

Dear Father, an empty shell—that's all that was left of the home after the packing and truck loading were completed. An empty shell...that's what I am without You. There's no warmth, no touch, no character. Today, I thank You for moving in and for living in my heart. May others who observe my life see a warm glow and know that yes, indeed, someone...Someone greater and higher lives here. *Amen.*

◇◇◇◇

Dear Father of Compassion and Truth: I thank You for all the Samaritans who have blessed me in my life. They came alongside and poured out their compassion. They listened but didn't stop there. They applied first the wine and then the oil and continually directed me to You, the healer of all diseases. Father, I too long to be a Samaritan who takes notice of the weary along the way and effectively applies the wine of truth and pours on the oil of healing. *Amen.*

◇◇◇◇

Jesus, thank You for speaking not only to the woman at the well but also to me. You know my desire to be drinking water that's motivating and life-giving. Yet so often I try to draw water from my own well. Doing things my way, neglecting time alone with You, and getting wrapped up in earthly things instead of making the heavenly my priority. Thank You for listening, guiding, and urging me onward toward the well of life. *Amen.*

◇◇◇◇

Father, Lord of Heaven and Earth: I know that You are a wonderful, all-powerful, all-knowing, and all-seeing God. At times in my weariness, I fail to see it. Thank You for taking my hand and telling me how much You care. I know that You have allowed the ailment that I have for a reason, and I believe as long as You allow it, You are working at making me a better person because of it. The healing process is in Your hand, Father, and I trust You with it. Thank You that when I am weak, then You are strong. *Amen.*

◇◇◇◇

Loving Father in Heaven, thank You once again for Your Word, which is alive and is profitable for reproof, for correction, and for instruction in righteousness. May Your Word be a part of my life in such a way that others can tell I've been with You. May You continue perfecting me and equipping me for every good work. *Amen.*

◇◇◇◇

Dear Father, my Father who cares and sees: as I focus on servanthood, I'm moved. Father, how often I fail and come short of Your glory. Thank You for sending Jesus to suffer on the cross, die, and rise again victoriously. I know, Father, that that is the only way to victory. Giving You my all and realizing that of myself, there's no good. It's only the new life in You that enables me to be a true servant. Thank You, Father, for reminding me, for loving me, and for urging me onward in servanthood. *Amen.*

◇◇◇◇

Dear Father, thank You for caring for Elijah way back there as he sat exhausted in the wilderness. That means You'll care for me in the same way so many years later. Thank You for reminding me that hearing what I need to hear means slowing down and being still. I must admit, Father, that there's a tremendous amount of interfering going on down here. So I ask that You would spare me from getting so involved and distracted that Your still small voice is drowned out. Today, Father, I'll be listening. *Amen.*

5

The Hearts of the Children

Dear Father,

thank You for our children, who unknowingly inspire and urge me to a closer walk with You. May I never let them down, and may I be what they long to see in their mother—godly. Thank You for the gift of each of them. They play such a vital part in our lives and home. May Your Spirit flow freely through my husband and me, motivating our children to good works. *Amen.*

◇◇◇◇

Good morning, Father: thank You for the good night's rest, even though I was up twice with our little daughter. Thankfully, my quiet time hasn't been interrupted so far. But why should I pine if my peaceful moments are interrupted because I am a mother? Thank You, Father, for calling me to motherhood. I do enjoy it to the fullest. Having You in our midst gives me a new spark and a spring to my steps as I begin each day. The hugs from the children, all the "I love yous," the birthday card that is their own handiwork, the obedience and trust they pour out on us warms my heart. These are only part of the joys of the gift of mothering. This morning, Father, I pray that You make my calling and election sure. *Amen.*

◇◇◇◇

Dear Almighty Father, does my life reflect my little daughter's in relation to You? Do I drift off to sleep every evening, knowing my world is right because of You? Are You the first thing I think of when I wake up? And through the day, do I turn to You with my joys and sorrows? Father, may I be true to our little daughter by having You in the center of my life. Here's my hand, Father. *Amen.*

◇◇◇◇

Dear Heavenly Father, thank You for Your patience. May I follow Your example in patience, and may I do better in seeing my son's fears through his eyes, patiently leading him through the path with the ducks, even though it might be the seventh time.

Thank You for again taking my hand and leading me through the path I fear—a path that, to You, is only strewn with harmless ducks. *Amen.*

◇◇◇◇

Thank You, dear Father, for the glimpses we can glean of the woman with true godly character. May I follow the example of Anna—not leaving the temple (Your presence), praying without ceasing, fasting, remembering, and pondering on Your goodness and Your gift of redemption when I drift off to sleep and when I wake up in the morning. You know, Father, the inspiration it brings to my heart to witness the older women of our congregation and others who have weathered the storms. I watch as they train and teach their little ones, and come forth shining and victorious as the children walk in truth. Lord, thank You also that I'm not alone in this, but that my husband is always there listening and letting me cry on his strong shoulder and urging me onward. May the fruit of our labor not be in vain, but may our little ones grow to be godly men and women. *Amen.*

◇◇◇◇

Thank You, dear Father of Good Gifts. Thank You for opening my womb and letting me enjoy the riches of bringing forth souls into Your kingdom. This morning, I will again bring my little son and daughter to Your temple gate. They are Yours. You only gave them to my husband and me to love them, train them, and lead them back to You. May I ever be mindful that they really are not our own, but Yours for service. *Amen.*

◇◇◇◇

Dear Heavenly Father, thank You for convicting me of not taking time with our children, but rushing through the day trying to see how much work I could accomplish—not taking time to admonish, teach, and train like I should have. And as I deal with them, remind me that delayed obedience is not obedience at all. May I call sin, sin. I am humbled by how I have failed, and yet I marvel at their childlike trust in their mother. They never tire telling me in excitement of anything new and surprising that they discover or that is happening in their lives. They never cease telling me, "I love you." And their bear hugs are heartwarming.

Yes, two little souls to teach and train, two little souls to love and show the way, two little souls to bring back to You. Thank You, God, for these precious gifts. May we be true to our calling. *Amen.*

◇◇◇◇

Dear Holy Father of Heaven, thank You for the gift of our little ones, and may I, like Mary, present them to You. Not once, but daily committing them into Your care, giving them into Your hands, for after all, they are Yours. In claiming them as my own, I remain unclean and unholy before You. Thank You, Lord, for having them as Your own and only looking to us parents as Your servants. To bring them back to You on our own is far too great a work for any of us frail, incomplete parents. Thank You for promising me that You will gently lead those with young. *Amen.*

◇◇◇◇

Dear Heavenly Father, I'm moved! Thank You for Your goodness. Thank You for revealing to us the struggles in our children's hearts. I have failed so often in nagging, in complaining when they are at fault.

Remind me that sin is sin and has to be dealt with, yet let me not forget that underneath the actions, there are struggles that are real in their lives. Today I ask for an extra portion of Your wisdom, Your strength, and Your understanding in dealing with our little ones—that I could look beyond the actions and see what's happening in the heart. *Amen.*

◇◇◇◇

Dear Father, I need an extra portion of Your wisdom, Your understanding, and love in dealing with our little souls. Not wisdom of my own, not my own ideas, not my own understanding, but Yours. And You promised to give it to me liberally (James 1:5) if I only ask. Thank You for this experience in bringing me to my wits' end and making me aware that the beginning of Your wisdom is in fearing You. May I also today make a new beginning in momently depending and leaning fully on You. *Amen.*

◇◇◇◇

Dear Father in Heaven, thank You for the reminder of my little ones. Thank You for the fruit I see in their lives. Truly, even though our teaching and training does seem vain and fruitless at times, there is good showing through. May I never grow weary, but continue teaching and training line upon line, precept upon precept. *Amen.*

◇◇◇◇

Lord, Father of All, I need You. I need Your Spirit of wisdom, understanding, might, and counsel. Yesterday was a day not so desirable. The children squabbled, whined, and fretted, and my nerves felt tattered and worn. Until I dropped into bed at night, I felt like a failure as a mother. Thank You, Father, for those days in keeping me humble and reminding me anew that mothering on my own is a work in vain. But looking to You is where victory lies. Thank You for this new day. Thank You for letting me start anew. As the children wake, let them see Jesus in their mother. *Amen.*

◇◇◇◇

Dear Father, I am so blessed over and over. Your Word is so richly filled with direction, courage, and hope. In You, I find mothering a joy. You didn't place these precious souls in our care and leave it at that. You supplied us with a manual that gives direction step by step, moment by moment. May You continue leading my husband and me as we lead our children. *Amen.*

◇◇◇◇

Dear Father, thank You for the gift of our children. May they be blessed for adding so much joy and spark to our home in their enthusiastic outlook in life. I thank You also for answering our prayers. Without Your wisdom, child training is in vain. May we never look at children as rebellious without trying to understand what's going on in their heart. I'm also humbled and moved that they do count time with Mother so important. May I be true to my calling of motherhood in depending on Your wisdom, Your understanding, Your discernment, Your strength, and Your love. *Amen.*

◇◇◇◇

Dear Father: As I rock the cradle of our little ones, may it be a fruitful experience because of You. As our children grow older, may they have a true desire to live a life of denying self, the world, and its lusts. May the children find it easy to follow us as we follow You. *Amen.*

◇◇◇◇

Almighty Righteous Father, thank You for Your detailed book of instructions on how to train up our children. You didn't give us this weighty work and then make us guess at what works. Thank You also for the mothers that have diligently heeded Your instruction, whose children have risen above their own selfish nature and chosen to give their whole lives to You. Father, our children are yet so small, so innocent, and moldable. I feel unlearned and inexperienced. Make me Your student in child training. So many little decisions rise throughout the day, yet I find it rewarding to see the freeing that's brought to my little ones when I do things Your way. *Amen.*

◇◇◇◇

Dear Father in Heaven, this morning I'm moved by Hannah's dedication in bringing her little Samuel back to You. No doubt her all was poured out to You as she looked to You for guidance, direction, and wisdom. Father, this morning I confess that too often in the grind of life—the squabbles to settle, the messes to clean—I forget the weighty work You have called me to. May my children know by my life that I have lent them to You as long as they live. How my heart yearns to see our sons and daughters grow up to be in favor with both God and man. *Amen.*

◇◇◇◇

Dear Father, thank You for the Bible, Your instructions on all areas of life. As a mother, child training is very near to my heart. Only once do I have an opportunity to teach my children of Your ways, only once are they so small and moldable. Only once, then the opportunity is gone. Father, impress on my heart the urgency in nurturing and admonishing. And again I thank You for Your direction as one by one, moment by moment, You direct my steps as we direct the steps of our little ones. Doing it Your way brings joys to motherhood. I am humbled over and over at the children's willing response. Today may You bless each of them in a special way. *Amen.*

◇◇◇◇

Dear Father of Love, You give and You take. For our dear friends, they had rocked their little one, hugged him good night, and soothed his ouchie for the last time. Then he was gone forever. Father, how final! So far beyond words! I can only try to imagine the pain and loss they must have felt. This time You had chosen them. What a stark reminder that we are not promised our children tomorrow. Only this moment we have to love and to hold. May I remember as we kiss our little ones good night that this could be the last time. Lord, not our will, but Yours be done. *Amen.*

◇◇◇◇

Dear Father of Love and Infinite Understanding: for us to understand why little ones must grow up without a mother is beyond us. And yet we believe that You are good. Yes, Father, I too am a mother. I love my dear little ones. But do I convey it so they can feel it? Do they know I'm there for their good? Am I praying about their tomorrows? Alone. Lord, that's what the little one felt. *Alone* is such a sad word. Jesus, I thank You that You know all about that word. You understand, You know, and what's more, You heal. Lord, my prayer is that our little ones may never have to experience the meaning of *alone*. Lord, my calling is weighty. It's too great for me. I cannot—but You can and I will let You. *Amen.*

◇◇◇◇

Father, as I fall before You, I am humbled, humbled at how easy it is for me to get discouraged at little things our children battle with—when You have for so many years ever so patiently taken my hand and listened, reassured, and comforted me. The fears that were ever so real to me were in reality nothing to be afraid of. You never gave up. You were never discouraged and never changed. May I be that to my children, a reflection of You. May we comfort with the same comfort we have been comforted with. *Amen.*

◇◇◇◇

Dear Father, thank You for being a Father who under-
stands and listens, but does not overlook sin. I have
failed so often. Our daughter needed instruction and
direction, not a frustrated mother. May You continually remind me that I am a mother, and may I live
up to my calling. This morning, I recommit my life
to You as a mother. I take the responsibility on myself
anew that I'm called to spend time with my children—
precept upon precept, line upon line, here a little and
there a little. *Amen.*

◇◇◇◇

Dear Father, I thank You for Your Word and the sim-
plicity You use in teaching me about You. I thank You
that You are always there for me and my good. As
much as I delight in giving my children what is best
and seeing them being nurtured, loved, and taken
care of, so much more You delight in seeing me pros-
pering and growing to new heights. So often, Father,
I simply forget to ask when I am in need of direction. I can visualize You waiting ever so patiently hoping, hoping, that I remember to look to You and ask.

Father, this morning, I ask that You would give me direction and wisdom in how to deal effectively with our little ones, who are struggling to play together peacefully. And, Father, if we are somehow neglecting any of their needs or are in any way wronging them, convict us of such. Thank You, Father. *Amen.*

◇◇◇◇

Dear Father, thank You for our little son, who at times puzzles me, frustrates me, yet continually delights me. So many times I sigh and scold at the tracks he leaves behind. Especially since it's thawing outside and there seemingly is no end to muddy boots, wet socks, and splashed trousers. Thank You, Father, for reminding me that all too soon our little son will be grown and the things that he treasures now will lose their value as he grows into adulthood. May I constantly be reminded that the way I relate to my little son as a mother will make a difference in what he treasures as a man. *Amen.*

◇◇◇◇

Dear Father, thank You for sending two little angels into our home, because of whom I have the privilege of being called a mother. Thank You for the many lessons they teach me. You see my desire to not only listen with my ears but with my heart also. And may I stoop low enough so as to see things through their eyes. Thank You, Father, for always dealing with me as a daughter, for being plenteous in mercy and slow to anger. Your love, patience, and endurance overwhelm my heart. Continue teaching me as I teach our little ones. *Amen.*

◇◇◇◇

Dear Father, thank You for the Bible, Your Word, which is full of direction and instruction for every area of our life. Thank You for this gift. We can always fall back on it, no matter what we face. You know my desire to work effectively this summer with the children and make their vacation a special one. You know my desire to mother in such a way that makes it a pleasure for our children to please me in all things. May our relationship be strengthened as I continue instilling in their little minds the need for prompt obedience and living an upright life, pleasing their Master in all things. *Amen.*

◇◇◇◇

Good morning, Good Shepherd: thank You for being my shepherd, for leading me, going before me, keeping me, knowing me, and most of all, dying for me and giving me life and giving it abundantly. In Your care, I feel safe, secure, and well cared for, and as I reflect on Your protection and shepherding, I wonder why I ever become fearful. Father, as I reflect on my shepherding of my children, I long to convey Your love in yet a deeper way. *Amen.*

◇◇◇◇

Father, as I sit here and ponder and meditate, my heart is awed and moved to soberness. Thank You for reminding me anew that my decisions do have lasting effects on our children. It mattered in Lot's time…when he chose to live near Sodom…and it still matters. Father, strengthen me, establish me, and settle me, so that I will never stray from Your path and protection. I know that staying under my husband's and Your protection will create a protection for our little ones. Thank You for being faithful. *Amen.*

◇◇◇◇

Dear Father, as I come before You in spirit and in truth, I am again awed at Your greatness and at the same time humbled by my own inadequacy. Thank You for teaching me anew, how I am nothing of myself, and how vain it is trying to use my wisdom, my understanding, and my ability. May I look to You for my all as I continue leading our little ones back to You. *Amen.*

◇◇◇◇

Dear Father, thank You for Your gentle ways with me. You suffer long with me, You patiently teach me step by step. You always have time to listen. You never despair of me, even though I fail so often. Father, that's what I long to pass on to our dear little ones. May I see through their eyes and remember that they are not yet grown like me. They are yet so small, so tender and innocent. Help me to look to You each moment of the way; may that produce a gentle touch. *Amen.*

6
The Bond of Marriage

Thank You, dear Father,

for giving me the blessing of having a faithful man, for the gift of a partner who has a heart after You. May I be a wife in whom the heart of my husband can safely trust, and may I do my husband good and not evil all the days of my life. And may I always from a true heart respect my husband for the man God created him to be. *Amen.*

◇◇◇◇

Dear Father, thank You for being good. Your plan and Your order in everything are so perfect. Thank You for the reminder anew that I was created to be my husband's helpmeet. So often I get weary and bowed down with mothering duties, and my husband gets what's left over. I pray that, as I start each day, You will impress deep in my heart that, because of my husband, I was created—and that I would make that purpose my priority and be giving him my all, meeting his needs, following his desires. Being in Your order brings great blessings, I know. May our children grow up with pleasant memories of their mother being *for* their father. *Amen.*

◇◇◇◇

Dear Heavenly Father, thank You for Your faithfulness in the journey to oneness of my husband and me, in blending of body, mind, and soul. Together, we echo the words of Samuel: "Thus far the LORD has helped us" (1 Samuel 7:12). May I continue to be faithful to my dear husband, living in obedience and submission lest Your Word be spoken ill of (Titus 2:5). Thank You also for the gift of a faithful God-fearing husband, who ministers to and shelters our household. *Amen.*

◇◇◇◇

Lord, as I pause and ponder our years of marriage, I'm overwhelmed by Your faithfulness. There have been so many areas where I was blind to my own selfishness, causing my husband unnecessary suffering. Yet I praise You for the path You have taken us in blending our lives in one. Truly marriage is a journey, and I trust You will lead us onward. I look forward to spending many more years with my faithful husband. Thank You for blessing us abundantly. *Amen.*

◇◇◇◇

Dear Heavenly Father, thank You for opening my eyes to some of the blind areas in my life. I had been praying that You would reveal anything in my life that is displeasing to You. And I was even human enough to be hurt how You went about convicting me. I'm sorry, Father. Thank You for forgiving me and loving me enough to bring it to my attention. Thank You for an understanding husband who is here for my good, always patient and forgiving. May You bless him richly, and may I, because of You, be a better wife. *Amen.*

◇◇◇◇

Dear Father, thank You for Your teaching on how we are to live with our husbands. I have found it a joy, a blessing, and a protection to live with my husband as You ordained. I have also been inspired to see the blessings of women following Your command while their husbands were walking outside Your order. You make a way for every step—yes, I believe it would be hard but not impossible, and the blessing would be great. *Amen.*

◇◇◇◇

Heavenly Father of Love, thank You for the gift of my husband. May You bless him for the blessing he has been to me, for his unselfish, gentle, and patient ways in dealing with me and the children. I know I have hurt him many times with my forward nature, but I thank You that You have been teaching me step by step, and I'm finding a great blessing in living under his protection. Truly marriage is a mystery—two souls blending and becoming one in mind, body, and soul. I believe that a God-ordained marriage—the husband and wife living together in humility, both giving their all for the other—is one of the greatest beauties You created. May my life as a wife be a virtuous one and a true crown to my husband. *Amen.*

◇◇◇◇

Father in Heaven, thank You for a husband to lean on at times like this, when the days are rough and it seems the children do nothing but fuss and I'm weary—weary of being a mother. But when my husband comes home from work, all seems well again. And I know that after the children are asleep, he is always willing to listen when I need to talk. May You bless him richly for the many times he pauses to thank me how I handled a situation with the children. Knowing he trusts me and my abilities to care for our little ones while he's gone gives me courage to go on. Thank You also for the gift and closeness we share in being able to pray together before we close the day for another night's rest. *Amen.*

◇◇◇◇

Dear Heavenly Father, thank You for being God and having power over all powers. This morning, I pause to thank You for the gift of a loving husband who has a heart after You. Thank You also for the example he is in forgiving. Many times, I have failed him, and yet his trust in me does wonders. Thank You for the relationship we share, my husband and I. There was a lot of pain involved in coming to where we are now. But thank You for the purifying that marriage brings. The beauty of husband and wife blending in body, mind, and soul is something that far surpasses understanding. Thank You for that gift. *Amen.*

◇◇◇◇

Dear Father, thank You for showing us through Jesus what submission is. This morning, I also thank You for the gift of a God-fearing husband who not only tells us, but shows us by example what he desires to see in me and our children. *Amen.*

◇◇◇◇

Dear Father: I take this moment to thank You for the relationship my husband and I share. There's no one on earth that we share a closer relationship with than each other. There is beauty in sharing the depths of our hearts, dreams, struggles, and tears, and knowing that we are there for the good of the other. Yes, at times, we do fail. Only last night, we hit a rough spot, but through communication, tears, and prayer, we move forward, knowing that in times like these we grow the most, and in times like these our love is strengthened anew—and once again we meet each other and You with a new zeal. May I remain faithful to You "all my days," which will result in being faithful to my husband and children. *Amen.*

◇◇◇◇

Dear Heavenly Father, thank You for forgiving, for lifting weary hands and feeble knees. I hang my head in shame for once again giving in to my flesh. You know my desire to be a true helpmeet, one who is always working toward strengthening my husband and not wearying him in any way. May You bless him for all he does for me, for being true to me, and for not growing weary when I, as his wife, fail him again. May I rise and look to You as my all, and may I continually be reminded to focus on my husband's strong points and love him. May my life be a witness that I am walking in the Spirit. *Amen.*

◇◇◇◇

Dear Father in Heaven, thank You for being all-powerful and also for ordaining powers under You. Everyone is accountable to a higher head. I thank You for anointing my husband as my head. May I see the seriousness of looking to him as my ordained authority. May You pour rich blessings upon him for being true to You in looking to You and the church as his head, and in return, being true to me. *Amen.*

◇◇◇◇

Father, I thank You for the gift of a God-fearing husband. As much as we don't want to hurt each other, we still do at times because we are human. I thank You that we can always ask forgiveness for our wrongs. I cherish the beauty of growing together as husband and wife, forbearing, forgiving, and lifting each other up. Where one is weak, the other is strong. Even though the one we love the most can hurt us the most, they can also help us the most. Thank You for choosing my husband to be mine. *Amen.*

◇◇◇◇

Thank You, Father in Heaven, for the many blessings You have bestowed and are bestowing upon us. As I reflect on our nine years of marriage, my heart overflows with praise. It definitely hasn't been thorn-free or pain-free. But Your love and faithfulness are reflected in all we've gone through—and truly our love has been strengthened and our faith increased, and we move forward in confidence and peace, thanking You that You've brought us this far, and knowing without a doubt that You'll continue. *Amen.*

7
Drawing Closer to God

Dear Father,

thank You for Your work on the cross, that through Jesus I am now called a saint. I ask that You convict me of anything in my life that is displeasing to You. May I daily continue to grow more in Your likeness. *Amen.*

◇◇◇◇

Father, thank You for the privilege of letting me live with You daily. Through studying Your Word, I learn what Your likes and dislikes are, and what makes You happy or sad. Thank You, Father, for adopting me into Your family. It brings a security I wouldn't know how to live without. *Amen.*

◇◇◇◇

Dear Heavenly Father, Father of Victories, thank You for again reminding me that my job is not to fight, but to follow the example of David and Jonah in crying out to You, seeking You, knocking, calling on You, and asking. You are the one who fights, You are the one who delivers and sets me free of each battle. Thank You for giving me the joy that goes with belonging to such a great warrior. I have no doubt that if I do the asking, You will still do the winning. *Amen.*

◇◇◇◇

Lord, may I be sensitive to Your Spirit and act when You are urging me to show a lost soul the way, whether it might be in sharing Your goodness, maybe just holding their hand, or perhaps interceding in prayer. Lord, may I be found faithful! *Amen.*

◇◇◇◇

Dear Jesus, thank You for taking me—this lifeless branch—and providing a way that I can be grafted to the true vine. May I be found abiding. May I remain stable and fixed in a state of bearing rich fruit. *Amen.*

◇◇◇◇

Thank You, Jesus, for all the admonishing and teaching You gave to me through Your Word before You went to Heaven. May I be careful to heed Your teachings and warnings, especially in the importance of knowing You. May I come to know You in yet a deeper way as I move forward. *Amen.*

◇◇◇◇

Thank You, dear Heavenly Father, that it's the lowly in heart You seek after. I also thank You that I don't have to have a high, noticeable position for Your approval; neither do I have to be popular to have a purpose-filled life. In fact, in Your eyes, I'm to have no power at all except Yours. Thank You for not being a respecter of persons but that You delight in me, not because of who I am, but simply as an act of love on Your part. To me, it doesn't matter how I look in the eyes of others. I am happy and content as long as I am in Your bosom, protected under Your wing. It's heartwarming and heavenly to look into Your eyes and see them filled with tenderness and care. In You, I can handle anything. In You, I'm secure. *Amen.*

◇◇◇◇

Dear Father, Lord of Heaven and Earth, thank You that You are sovereign, that You are above all and in all. This morning, I thank You for allowing things in my own life to simply go backward. It seems like my own resources are failing in the smallest details of my life. It makes me realize how weak and frail I am of myself. I need You, I need Your power, I need Your strength. Really, it's Your love and goodness that allow my little world to crumble. You are about to bring me to fuller dependence on You, to see my own sinfulness. Lord, it makes me grasp anew Your words through the apostle: "When I am weak, then I am strong." Thank You. *Amen.*

◇◇◇◇

Thank You, dear Heavenly Father, for sending Jesus, who is God in bodily form, and yet at the same time, Your Son. Thank You for the work You have done in my life so that circumstances no longer control me and make me angry like they used to; now I can see You more and more in everything, in all circumstances. Yes, Jesus, You are more than Joseph's son.

You are the Son of the living God. Truly You are the Anointer, the Healer—You return sight to the blind, and You free the captives. *Amen.*

◇◇◇◇

Dear Loving Heavenly Father, my Father whom I trust and depend on so much: You are my all, my only hope, my inspiration. Thank You for all the strange things You've done in my life. Truly, I was dead and You brought me to life. You've healed, You've transformed, You've worked and chiseled; and I ask that You continue doing just that until You've prepared me to meet You face-to-face. And as long as I linger, may I never cease glorifying Your name for what You've done and what You will continue doing. *Amen.*

◇◇◇◇

Dear Jesus, at times I feel so distant from You and I don't know why. I try reading, studying, and meditating, but I'm not moved like usual. I say my prayer, but nothing changes. But I see now that You want me to be honest. You want me to tell You exactly how I

feel. Already I feel better as I pour out my all on You.
Thank You for Your comforting, gentle voice. You
asked me to just rest in You—don't try to accomplish
things on my own. It's in abiding, not in doing. Thank
You, Jesus! I will do just that. *Amen.*

◇◇◇◇

Dear Father, Mighty Father in Heaven, thank You for
the explicit directions that You give me in living for
You. You didn't just make me guess…You left me step-
by-step directions and a true example. What warms
my heart so is that in truly delighting in You, You
give me my heart's desire. For my desire is to line up
with Yours. What a joy in serving You, my Father of
Delight. *Amen.*

◇◇◇◇

Dear Father, I'm so pleased to be part of Your habitation. The longer I live there, the more familiar I
become with You and Your ways. At first, when
I came to dwell with You, I was fearful. At times, I
quivered and shook—but yes, truly, I've come a long

way. No longer are You someone to fear, but someone who's full of love and compassion, someone who
convicts and forgives. I have found Your habitation
to be a comfort, a refuge, a strong tower, a peaceful
dwelling. And thank You that though I will someday
leave my earthly dwelling, Your dwelling remains forever. *Amen.*

◇◇◇◇

Dear Faithful Father, thank You for answering my
prayer. Truly if I ask You to fight, and then stay out
of Your way, the battle is always victorious. May You
bless the children for doing their part in making it a
blessed day. Thank You for those times when I again
realize that on my own I can't; instead, it's leaning on
You where the victory lies. *Amen.*

◇◇◇◇

Lord, Father of All, thank You for the example You
are to us, always choosing the lowest place. When
Jesus, Your only Son, was born, You could have chosen the greatest mansion, but instead You chose the

lowly stable out back. That in itself reveals Your very nature. Really, Lord, I find it a joy knowing that my Savior, my King and Lord, was born in such a lowly state. Thank You for teaching us over and over that to be the greatest, we must become the least, and that to be exalted is to be humbled. To become Your child, we must become nothing. That's my desire, Father, to become nothing as to manifest Your greatness. *Amen.*

◇◇◇◇

Dear Father of Comfort, at this time I'm facing some sore testings. My first impulse when I faced up to what was happening was to flinch: *pain…no, Lord.* But oh, the sweetness in accepting and resting in Your arms knowing You are in charge. I will look to You, the author and finisher of this trial. My desire is that You would have Your way and that I would in no way muddle the situation by panicking and taking things into my own hands. Thank You, Father, for this trial. I welcome it knowing that it is for our good in refining us and bringing us close to You. *Amen.*

⬦⬦⬦

Dear Father, Father of Love and Light: I thank You for listening to my cry and convicting me and reminding me to stay close. I marvel at Your goodness and how ready and willing You are to answer my prayers. I am humbled at Your love toward me. You care about every detail, and You are even more concerned about my well-being than I am. Thank You for the promise of Your protection if I remain close enough to hear Your heartbeat. May I refocus in giving You my all, lest my house be desolate. *Amen.*

⬦⬦⬦

Dear Father of Good Gifts, thank You for the many gifts You have bestowed on our family. Yet I recognize all that we have is Yours. We are only Your servants, and all fruit that we bear is because of You, the strong vine. I know I have already stolen from You, as did Gehazi, Elisha's servant. I have kept honor for myself that belonged to You. At times, pride creeps in, and again, I'm tempted to claim honor for myself. Lord, Father, may it be far from me. And as I continue to draw closer to You, I continue to see my unworthiness—that of myself, I am nothing. It's just because of You Lord, that I am what I am. *Amen.*

◇◇◇◇

Dear Father in Heaven, thank You for all the detailed instructions You give me in Your Word. It is so plain and simple. It takes no college degree or higher education, but instead being in tune with Your Spirit and depending on You for guidance and direction. You give us the power to rise to higher planes. Continue, Father, to teach me this holy art, continue to clear my vision as I fill the role of a wife and mother. May my faith remain alive so that I would believe all You have said. For it is only in You that I have life, power, and purpose. *Amen.*

◇◇◇◇

Father in Heaven, Father of Hope and Life: once more I am invigorated, strengthened, and lifted up. Last night, I went to bed feeling defeated and discouraged, and that's how I woke up this morning. I fail so often. And spending time with You alone was hard to do with pressing cares and reaching out to others. Father, I realize anew that it's those who realize they can't whom You delight in helping up and onward. Truly, my burden is lighter and my spirit renewed as I fall at Your feet and realize that I can't, but You can, and I will let You. *Amen.*

⬦⬦⬦⬦

Jesus, thank You for Your example in showing me how important it is to spend time in prayer. The next time I'm tempted to get my "much needed rest," gently whisper, "Could you not watch with Me one hour?" *Amen.*

⬦⬦⬦⬦

Dear Father in Heaven, I thank You for being the Creator of Heaven and Earth. Your wonderful works, who can declare them? I thank You that You have created this earth—a little heaven for us to enjoy as we pass through in preparation to enter our real home, Heaven. I thank You for the gift of life. I truly have learned to enjoy being here. For at this moment, this is exactly where You want me to be. So teach me to slow down and take minute vacations as I joyfully go about my calling as a wife to my husband, as a mother to my children, and as a sister in the church, knowing that in You I am secure, loved, cherished, and well taken care of; and that nothing will happen to me that has not first passed Your approval. *Amen.*

◇◇◇◇

Dear Father in Heaven, I thank You for again helping me to see that facing pain and hurts is okay. And that You are not allowing it because You delight in seeing me suffer; instead, You are after making me more like You. I do believe that all that happens in my life is for my good and Your glory. Thank You for the comfort You sent to me at just the right time in reminding me that You are here for me. And it's okay to hurt. Thank You for tears, which are healing to my soul. Thank You for being all-powerful—thank You that You have the power to turn the worst evil into something good. *Amen.*

◇◇◇◇

Dear Father, how often have I tried to beautify my acts by my own good works? I want my life to taste good to others when all You want is just me, my sins and all. In return, You have given me Your life, Your love, Your joy, and Your peace. May my life in You be a sweet-smelling savor to You and to all those around me. *Amen.*

◇◇◇◇

Dear Heavenly Father, thank You for being good. Thank You for not asking of me to understand all You do, but only asking that I trust and believe that all You do and allow in my life is for my good and to the bettering of Your kingdom. May I now not only *tell* our children that we need not understand; may my life *show* that I trust and don't continue to try to figure things out. Thank You for being God, for being in control and freeing me. *Amen.*

◇◇◇◇

Dear Heavenly Father, You are altogether wonderful, and Your ways past finding out. Thank You for giving me the desire of my heart, for drawing me closer. Thank You for doing it Your way. The drawing closer was so much more meaningful and the lesson so much sweeter since You gave it to me not as I had planned, but as You saw best. May I be reminded that You are at work all the time in drawing me closer. Thank You, Father! *Amen.*

◇◇◇◇

Heavenly Father, thank You for taking pleasure in my well-being. Thank You for being my Master. It is such a joy—actually exciting and thrilling to wake up each morning and remember that You take pleasure in having a relationship with me. That father–daughter relationship is far greater and sweeter than any earthly riches there are. Thank You for causing me to be prosperous. *Amen.*

◇◇◇◇

Dear Jesus, thank You for showing Yourself freely, continually in my life. Because of Your faithfulness in my life, I no longer fear in being in Your presence. Instead I have come to enjoy those encounters with You, whether they are times of rebuke, exhortation, or reproof (2 Timothy 4:2). I have the confidence they're for my benefit and Your glory. And just being in Your presence, under Your protection, brings a great security and creates a special bond. *Amen.*

◇◇◇◇

Thank You, Heavenly Father, for being true. My heart is overflowing with gratitude and thanksgiving, for truly I have heard and seen exactly what You have told me. My Savior lives, He died and rose again victorious, and He is now at Your right hand interceding on my behalf. I'm free, I'm redeemed through His blood. And now through repentance, I have entered Your kingdom. May my heart never cease glorifying and praising You. *Amen.*

◇◇◇◇

Dear Father, thank You for being my Father, for really caring about what's troubling me, for listening to me, for convicting and comforting me. Again, I realize anew that You are the answer to all troubled seas. If I stop to listen, You do speak and You do make a difference. Today, Father, I trust that Your kingdom work will be my first priority. If the lawn doesn't get mowed, it will patiently wait; if the weeds don't all get pulled today, they will still be there tomorrow. You promised to *add all these things* and I trust You will—maybe not in my way, but in Yours. *Amen.*

◇◇◇◇

Dear Father, thank You for seeking me continually. Who am I that You desire a relationship with me? Yet it is of great importance to You. It is such a comfort knowing that not only am I seeking You but that You are also seeking me, so really abiding in Your presence is not difficult or impossible at all. Thank You, Father, for seeking me. *Amen.*

Dear Jesus, You know how much I long to see You and how lonesome I get for You. And how much I long to give You a gift…something costly to show You how much You mean to me, for giving Your life for me. Thank You for reminding me that I have something valuable that I can give to You daily…my life. At this moment, Jesus, I recommit my life to You. Today, remind me that, as circumstances arrive, my hopes, my dreams, my pride, my self—my all—it's Yours. These are now no longer mine but Yours to use and do with as You see fit. *Amen.*

To learn more about other books in
the Plain Living collection, as well as
other Harvest House books, and to read
sample chapters, visit our website:

www.harvesthousepublishers.com

HARVEST HOUSE PUBLISHERS
EUGENE, OREGON